Collins

Student's Book

Real Lives
Real Listening
Intermediate B1–B2

Sheila Thorn

Collins

HarperCollins Publishers
77-85 Fulham Palace Road
Hammersmith
London W6 8JB

Originally published in 2009 as three separate titles:
Real Lives, Real Listening: My Family
Real Lives, Real Listening: A Typical Day
Real Lives, Real Listening: A Place I Know Well
by The Listening Business www.thelisteningbusiness.com

Subsequently published by North Star ELT in 2011.

This new edition combining all three titles was published in 2013 by HarperCollins Publishers Ltd

Reprint   10 9 8 7 6 5 4 3 2 1 0

© HarperCollins Publishers Ltd 2013

The right of **Sheila Thorn** to be identified as the Author of this Work has been asserted by the Publisher in accordance with the Copyright, Designs and Patents Act 1988.

ISBN 978-0-00-752232-3

Collins® is a registered trademark of HarperCollins Publishers Limited

www.collinselt.com

A catalogue record of this book is available from the British Library.

Printed in China by South China Printing Co. Ltd

All rights reserved. No part of this book may be reproduced, stored in a retrieval system, or transmitted in any form or by any means, electronic, mechanical, photocopying, recording or otherwise, without the prior permission in writing of the Publisher. This book is sold subject to the conditions that it shall not, by way of trade or otherwise, be lent, re-sold, hired out or otherwise circulated without the Publisher's prior consent in any form of binding or cover other than that in which it is published and without a similar condition including this condition being imposed on the subsequent purchaser.

HarperCollins does not warrant that www.collinselt.com or any other website mentioned in this title will be provided uninterrupted, that any website will be error free, that defects will be corrected, or that the website or the server that makes it available are free of viruses or bugs. For full terms and conditions please refer to the site terms provided on the website.

Photos on pages 8 and 9 © Wolfgang. Photo of Jill in Unit 14 © Sheila Thorn. All other images are from Shutterstock.

Free teacher's notes and answer keys available online at:
www.collinselt.com

Contents

Introduction		6

My Family

Unit 1   **Tecwyn**   8
Tecwyn is originally from North Wales, but he emigrated to Canada in his 20s. He now lives in Vancouver, on the west coast of Canada.

Unit 2   **Yasmin**   22
Yasmin was born in Pakistan but her family emigrated to England when she was a child. She now lives in Huddersfield, in northern England.

Unit 3   **Scott**   36
Scott comes from Australia and is currently working in London for a few years before returning there.

Supplementary Units

Unit 4   **Carol**   48
Carol comes from Dublin, the capital of the Republic of Ireland. She now lives in a small coastal town in Essex, in southeastern England.

Unit 5   **Barbara**   56
Barbara lives in Paderborn in northern Germany. Her husband is from Chile and Barbara speaks fluent Spanish and English.

A Typical Day

Unit 6   **Andrew**   64
Andrew is from East London. He is a psychology student at Birmingham University, but he is currently spending a gap-year gaining work experience.

Unit 7	**Tammy**	78
	Tammy comes from Canada, but she now lives in east London where she is a senior theatre nurse in a busy hospital.	
Unit 8	**Caroline and Martin**	92
	Caroline and Martin both do backstage theatre work in London. They met while they were studying to become theatre technicians at RADA (the Royal Academy of Dramatic Art).	

Supplementary Units

Unit 9	**Anne**	112
	Anne comes from the Midlands in the UK, but she recently moved to the Greek island of Crete where she works as a holiday rep for a British travel operator.	
Unit 10	**Fernand**	122
	Fernand comes from Belgium but he is currently working at a gentleman's club in central London.	

A Place I Know Well

Unit 11	Scott	132
Unit 12	Ingse	144
	Ingse comes from Bergen in Norway, but she has lived, worked and studied in the UK and Germany.	
Unit 13	Anne	160

Supplementary Units

Unit 14	Jill	174
	Jill comes from North Wales but she now lives in London. She has lived and worked abroad, most recently in California.	
Unit 15	Barbara	184

Teacher's notes and answer keys available online at: www.collinselt.com

About the author

The author, Sheila Thorn, is an experienced teacher and materials writer with a particular interest in authentic listening. She is the founder of The Listening Business: www.thelisteningbusiness.com

Acknowledgements

Books, articles, lectures and workshops by the following people have been invaluable in helping me to develop the approach to authentic listening I have used in the *Real Lives, Real Listening* series: Gillian Brown, Ron Carter, Richard Cauldwell, John Field, Jennifer Jenkins, Tony Lynch, Mike McCarthy, Shelagh Rixon, Michael Rost, Paul Seligson, Adrian Underhill, Mary Underwood, Penny Ur and J.J. Wilson.

My grateful thanks to the following people and institutions for commenting on and piloting these materials:

Maria Sforza and Heather Wansbrough-Jones at *South Thames College, London*, Carol Butters, Sarah Dearne, Michelle Parrington and Justin Sales at *Stevenson College, Edinburgh*, Jonathan Fitch at *The Oxford English Centre*, Hazel Black and Chris Jannetta at *English for Everyone, Aberdeen*, Sasha Goldsmith at *Rands English Language Tuition*, Elizabeth Stitt at the *University of St Andrews*, Sophie Freeman, Jen McNair Wilson, John Marquis, Harriet Williams and Jo Whittick at *English in Chester*, Dariana Cristea, Beverley Gray and Keith Harris at *Loughborough College*, Catherine Marshall and Michelle Scolari at *Bellerbys College, London*, Kath Hargreaves, Julia Hudson and Eric Smith at *Embassy CES, Oxford*, Andy Wright at *Queen Mary, University of London*, Zoe Smith at *OISE Bristol*, Elizabeth Bray and Mike Powell at *Coventry College*, Joe Ferrari at *Dundee College* and Julia Isidro at *Kings Oxford*.

I am also extremely grateful to all the people who kindly allowed me to interview them for these books, particularly those for whom English is not their first language.

This book is dedicated to my father and to Jill for their constant love, support and encouragement, and to my late, and greatly missed, mentor Jean Coles.

Introduction

Aims
The main aim of the *Real Lives, Real Listening* series is to provide busy teachers with ready-made listening materials which will effectively *train*, rather than just test, their students in listening. A parallel aim is to boost students' confidence in their listening skills by exposing them to authentic texts. A further aim is to introduce students to the grammatical structures and idiomatic expressions which are typically used in informal spoken English.

The series reflects the latest academic theories on the process of decoding listening input and the importance of authentic listening practice in language acquisition. The series also reflects our new awareness of the huge differences between spoken and written English highlighted by recent research on spoken English corpora.

Authenticity
Unlike the listening texts typically found in coursebooks, each text in *Real Lives, Real Listening* is 100% unscripted. This means that students are exposed to the features of spoken English which they encounter outside the classroom and generally find so daunting. These features include assimilation, elision, linking, weak forms, hesitations, false starts, redundancy and colloquial expressions.

The *Real Lives, Real Listening* series is carefully designed to include both native and near-fluent non-native English speakers, reflecting the fact that most of the English which is spoken these days is between non-native speakers of English.

Content
The series is at three levels: Elementary (A2), Intermediate (B1–B2) and Advanced (B2–C1), with 15 units for each level.

The books are divided into three sections: *My Family*, *A Typical Day* and *A Place I Know Well*. There are five units in each section. The first three contain a wide variety of focused exercises which the teacher can select from, depending on the needs of their students. These units are graded in terms of difficulty, from easier to more challenging. The final two units in each section are for revision purposes. Here the speakers recycle, naturally, the lexis and grammatical structures found in the previous three units. Every unit contains verbatim transcripts of the listening texts and useful glossaries.

Extensive piloting of these materials has shown that students at all levels experience a huge sense of achievement when they find they can actually understand a native or competent non-native speaker talking at a natural speed. The *Real Lives, Real Listening* series provides them with that opportunity.

Sheila M. Thorn

My Family

UNIT 1 Tecwyn

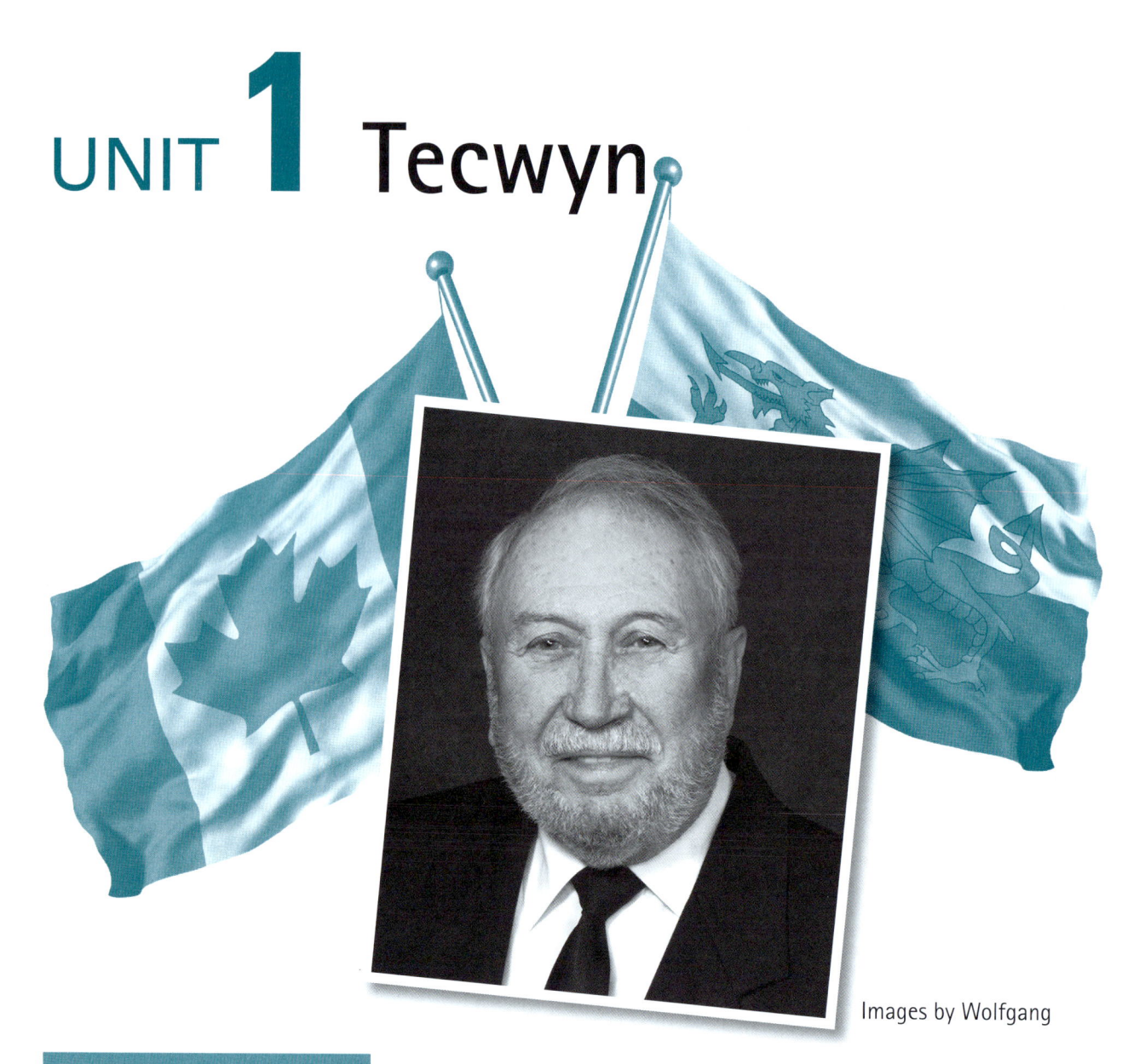

Images by Wolfgang

1. Pre-Listening Comprehension

A Schema building

Tecwyn was born in North Wales, but moved to Canada in the 1950s. How much do you know about Canada? Discuss the following statements with a partner and mark them True or False.

1. T F Canada is the second-largest country in the world in terms of area.
2. T F The population of Canada is around 60 million.
3. T F Nearly 25% of all the fresh water in the world is in Canada.
4. T F The largest city in Canada is Vancouver.
5. T F Forests cover about half of Canada.

My Family

B Discussion

Discuss the questions in small groups. Share your answers with the class.

1. What else do you know about Canada?
2. Think about some of the possible reasons Tecwyn decided to emigrate to Canada.
3. What do you think it must have been like to start a new life in Canada in the 1950s?

C Normalisation – Gap-fill

🎧 2 to 🎧 7

NOTE: The interview takes place on the phone, so there is quite a lot of background noise. You may find this unit rather challenging, and need to repeat the audio tracks to aid your comprehension.

This exercise is designed to help you get used to Tecwyn's voice. There is a word missing from the end of each excerpt. Try to guess the missing word and write it down. Then listen to tracks 2–7 to check your answers. How well did you guess?

1. I was there for four summers and five _____ .
2. It's a beautiful part of the _____.
3. His wife, like mine, never _____.
4. Where is she at the _____?
5. There's an Australian company that operates this Russian icebreaker which is also a research ship and which carries about 100 to 125 paying _____.
6. Her job is titled 'hotel _____'.

Images by Wolfgang

2. Listening Comprehension

A True/False

In this first exercise, Tecwyn talks about how he ended up in Vancouver. Listen and decide if each statement is True (T) or False (F). Remember to give reasons for your answers.

1. T F Tecwyn has two sons and two daughters.
2. T F Tecwyn's wife is half-Irish.
3. T F She moved to Canada during the war.
4. T F Tecwyn met his wife at work.
5. T F Tecwyn applied for a job with an Asian exchange bank.
6. T F Tecwyn spent some time in the Far East as a soldier.
7. T F On arriving in Canada, Tecwyn worked at his bank's head office for several months.
8. T F Tecwyn then asked if he could be transferred to Ottawa.
9. T F After three years in Ottawa, Tecwyn moved to Montreal.
10. T F After Montreal he spent the next five years in Winnipeg.
11. T F During one winter in Winnipeg the temperature stayed above -25C for a fortnight.
12. T F Tecwyn then went to work for a different bank in Vancouver.
13. T F Vancouver is Tecwyn's favourite city in Canada.
14. T F Tecwyn was in Vancouver at the time of this interview.
15. T F Tecwyn likes Vancouver because of the surroundings.
16. T F He says 'the long mainland' of British Columbia is probably the best place to live in Canada.

B Gap-Fill

Tecwyn talks about his eldest son. Before you listen, try to predict which words, or which types of words (nouns, adjectives, prepositions, parts of verbs, etc.) will fit in the gaps. Then listen and check your answers.

1. Tecwyn's two oldest children were _____ in Winnipeg.
2. Tecwyn's _____ son works for a pulp mill.
3. McKenzie is in _____ British Columbia.
4. Tecwyn's oldest son also installs _____ _____ in that area.
5. His son is very good at _____ things.
6. Before going to work in the pulp mill, Tecwyn's son worked for a _____ company.
7. Tecwyn says his son _____ turn his _____ to anything.

10 *My Family*

8. This son's _____ doesn't_____.
9. This son has four _____ aged____, ____, ____ and ____.

C Questions

Tecwyn talks about his two daughters. Listen and answer the questions.

1. What is Catherine's job?
2. Does she work for herself, or is she employed by a company full-time?
3. Where does Catherine live?
4. How long does it take Tecwyn to drive to Catherine's place?
5. How old are Catherine's children?
6. What does Tecwyn's younger daughter love doing?
7. Which company does this daughter work for?
8. During which part of the year does she work for this company?
9. What does she usually do the rest of the year?
10. How do you think the interviewer feels when she confuses the Arctic with the Antarctic?
11. What does the Australian company operate?
12. What is the second function of the ship?
13. How many paying passengers does the ship carry?
14. What is the daughter's job title?
15. How does Tecwyn describe this daughter?

D Gap-fill

Tecwyn talks about his youngest son and another relative. Before you listen, try to predict which words, or which **types** of words, will fit in the gaps. Then listen and check your answers.

1. Tecwyn's youngest son isn't _____.
2. He lives with a_____.
3. She is what is called a '_____ _____ wife' in Canada.
4. They have a _____-year-old son.
5. Tecwyn doesn't have any other _____ in Canada.
6. He has one _____ who lives in_____.
7. The interviewer has _____ her.
8. She's _____ than Tecwyn.

3. Interesting Language Points

A Using the present continuous to talk about the future

When Tecwyn tells the interviewer that his daughter is going to Antarctica in November, the interviewer replies by saying:

What's she doing down there?

We use the present continuous when we talk about what someone has arranged to do. Here are some more examples:

'What are you doing at the weekend?'
'Where are you going on holiday this year?'
'I'm meeting Sven at 5 o'clock.'
'I'm starting a new job on Monday.'

B Making deductions from the simple past

Tecwyn says:

. . . her father was English, her mother was Irish.

Because he uses the simple past, we know that they are no longer alive.

C The present perfect simple

Tecwyn says this about his daughter's love of travelling:

She's done it all.

He uses the present perfect simple here to show that in her life, up until now, she has travelled to a lot of different places around the world.

Later the interviewer asks about Tecwyn's youngest son and his partner. She says:

How long have they been together?

The interviewer uses the present perfect simple because she is talking about the period of time from when the couple met up until now.

D Using *will* to talk about habits

Tecwyn says this about his youngest daughter:

She works there from April till October, and then generally from November until the following April she'll travel anywhere in the world.

Tecwyn says *She'll travel* because he is talking about a regular habit.

12 *My Family*

Will is generally shortened to *'ll* in spoken English. Here are some more examples of this use of *will*:

> 'My sister normally works a ten-hour day, Monday to Thursday, then on Fridays <u>she'll take</u> the day off and spend it in the country.'

> 'My boyfriend sits in front of a computer all day at work and then in the evenings <u>he'll sit</u> in front of his computer at home and play computer games until midnight.'

E Using *must* to make deductions about the present

The interviewer says about Tecwyn's oldest son:

> *You must be very proud of him.*

We use *must* when we see something as logically true. In this case Tecwyn has talked about all the things his son can do, so it is logical for the interviewer to assume he is proud of his son. Here are some more examples of this use of *must*:

> Dina: *I didn't go to bed until 4 o'clock this morning!*
> Anna: *You must be very tired.*

> Sabir: *I haven't eaten anything since breakfast.*
> Alex: *You must be starving!*

> Miko: *My daughter has just passed her driving test.*
> Imran: *She must be thrilled.*

F Colloquial language

1. *Yep* instead of *Yes*
After the interviewer says 'that must have been a big step to go Canada', Tecwyn replies:

> *Yep, yep, it was.*

This use of *yep* for *yes* is very common in spoken English in the USA and Canada, but also amongst British native speakers to express definite agreement.

2. *Gosh!*
After Tecwyn tells the interviewer that his daughter is going to Antarctica, the interviewer replies:

> *Gosh! What's she doing up there?*

UNIT 1: *Tecwyn* 13

The word *Gosh!* usually with an exclamation mark (!) is used to express surprise, as in these examples:

Ramon: *Have you heard the latest? Paul's resigned.*
Maria: *Gosh! What happened?*

Kim: *I've just discovered a huge crack in my ceiling.*
Jean: *Gosh! Are you covered by insurance?*

3. *bloody*

When the interviewer asks if it is significant that Tecwyn said he spent four summers and five winters in Winnipeg, Tecwyn says 'Yeah'. When the interviewer asks why, Tecwyn says:

'Cos it's bloody cold!

In fact *bloody* is a swear word which is used for emphasis, as in the above example. It is also used to express frustration or exasperation, as in the following examples:

'I need to see the doctor, but I can't get a bloody appointment until next Friday.'
'I've got a bloody awful day tomorrow – meetings all morning and then a health and safety training session all afternoon.'
'Where's my bloody mobile phone? If I don't find it soon I'm going to miss the train.'

However, some people find the word *bloody* offensive and you should be careful about using it. The best advice is: 'If in doubt – don't!'

G Intonation patterns

1. Rising-falling intonation

When we give two different pieces of information in a sentence, our voice rises on the first piece of information and falls on the second piece of information. Listen again to Tecwyn:

Two of them were born in Winnipeg; two were born in Vancouver.

2. Falling intonation

When we are giving a number of pieces of information our voice falls on the final piece of information. Listen again to Tecwyn talking about his oldest son's children and note how his voice falls on nine:

His boys are 13, 12, 11 and nine.

14   *My Family*

4. Further Listening Practice

A Contractions

We use contractions in spoken English much more frequently than in written English. What are the contracted forms of the following items? How do you pronounce them?

> I am, you are, he is, she is, we are, they are,
> I have, you have, he has, she has, we have, they have,
> does not, do not

Now look at the following phrases and sentences taken from the interview and predict where Tecwyn or the interviewer use contractions.

1. a daughter who is 41
2. and it is a beautiful part of the world
3. we have got, you know, mountains, forests, seaside
4. we do not have those horrible winters
5. But that is two quite different things, is it not?
6. she is a world traveller
7. She will travel anywhere in the world.
8. What is she doing up there?
9. There is an Australian company that operates this Russian icebreaker.
10. oh, they have been together about four years
11. you have met her
12. She is younger than I am.

Now listen to the excerpts and check whether you predicted the correct contractions.

B Recognising sentence stress

Stressed words are the most important in spoken English because they carry the most meaning. Which words do you think Tecwyn stresses in the following extracts?

1. She spent the war years in Ireland.
2. we worked together in London
3. I applied to work for an Eastern Exchange Bank
4. I'd done a tour out in er, the Far East with the army
5. I was there for four summers and five winters.
6. Well, first of all it's the climate
7. And then generally, from November until the following April she'll travel anywhere in the world.
8. But er, this November she's, she has a job in Antarctica.

UNIT 1: *Tecwyn* 15

9. *There's an Australian company that operates this Russian icebreaker which is also a research ship.*
10. *She's sort of a people person.*

Now listen to find out if your predictions were correct.

C Assimilation

Canadians and Americans tend not to pronounce the *t* sound in certain words. Listen to these examples:

> *She has her own li<u>tt</u>le company.*
> *She lives in the Uni<u>t</u>ed States.*

This non-pronunciation of the *t* sound appears especially when

Canadians and Americans say numbers out loud. Listen to Tecwyn talking about his daughter's job on the icebreaker:

> *and which carries about a hundred to a hundred and twen<u>t</u>y-five paying passengers*

D Linking

When a word ends in a consonant in spoken English and the next word begins with a vowel, the end of the first word often links with the start of the second word, making it sound as if the two words are one.

Linking also occurs when the consonant at the end of one word is the same as the consonant at the start of the next word. Listen to these excerpts and mark where linking occurs. Then check the answers with your teacher.

1. *her father was English, her mother was Irish*
2. *She spent the war years in Ireland.*
3. *How did I get into banking?*
4. *That's sort of a long story, I guess.*
5. *I flew into Toronto . . .*
6. *What's so nice about it?*
7. *he also gets involved in all sorts of other stuff as well*
8. *She lives in the United States.*
9. *she looks after those passengers*
10. *She's sort of a people person.*

5. Further Language Development

A Extension exercise

Fill in the blanks in these new sentences with words you heard during Tecwyn's interview. The words are listed in the box to help you. One of the words is used twice.

> after   applied   bloody   care   divorced   do   got
> hand   involved   must   research   significant
> similarities   spent   technical   transferred   up   was

1. Have you _____ any children?
2. My grandfather _____ born in 1887.
3. Yesterday I _____ three hours on the phone trying to book a holiday.
4. Let's try and meet _____ in the summer, when the weather's better.
5. You said you're a nurse. What does your husband _____?
6. I always try not to get _____ in my brother's arguments with his wife.
7. I'm not very _____ – I just learned how to send text messages.
8. My sister can turn her _____ to anything. You name it, she can do it.
9. You _____ be exhausted – you've been working on that report for hours.
10. On Thursdays my mother takes _____ of the children and my husband and I spend the evening together.
11. My brother is _____, but he still sees his ex-wife.
12. I have just heard about some _____ that is being carried out into the effects of divorce on children.
13. Can you look _____ my cat while I'm on holiday?
14. The use of the voice is one of the _____ between teaching and acting.
15. I've _____ for a new job, but I don't know if I'll get it.
16. Last night there was a pile-up on the motorway, so I ended _____ not getting home till midnight.
17. My brother used to work in New York, but he's just heard he's being _____ to Croydon, so he's not very happy.
18. There has been a _____ rise in unemployment, according to reports.
19. Do you think you could you stop your _____ dog barking all night?

UNIT 1: *Tecwyn* 17

B Prepositions and adverbs

Insert the correct preposition or adverb in these sentences based on vocabulary taken from Tecwyn's interview:

1. We were supposed to meet _____ at 8, but my train was late so I didn't get there until quarter past.
2. I've applied _____ a job _____ a ferry.
3. It was my turn to cook last night, but I got home so late we ended _____ getting a takeaway pizza.
4. I haven't played tennis _____ years.
5. Mike's just heard he's being transferred _____ his company's New York office. He says he'll be really sad to leave London.
6. Simon's just been telling us _____ your holiday. It sounds fantastic.
7. I go to the gym about three times a week _____ average.
8. Our firm's involved _____ takeover talks at the moment, so I can't really take any time off.
9. I've been _____ the same firm since 2001.
10. His parents were so proud _____ him going to university that they bought him a car.
11. Don't worry about Petra – she can take care _____ herself.
12. Can you look _____ my bag while I nip to the loo?

C The present continuous, the present perfect simple and the simple past

Put the verbs in brackets into the present continuous, present perfect simple or simple past, as appropriate.

1. On no! I only (buy) _____ this milk on Tuesday and it's already gone off.
2. I (meet) _____ her a couple of times over the past few months.
3. We (go) _____ out for dinner last night to celebrate my pay rise.
4. We (save) _____ $1,000 deposit for a new apartment already.
5. We (see) _____ Brad at the party and he was asking after you.
6. David (pass) _____ his driving test last week, so now he (look) _____ for a cheap second-hand car.
7. Sorry for not getting in touch earlier, but I (lose) _____ my mobile phone so I (have) _____ to get your number from Andy.
8. I (get) _____ this DVD last week, but we (see) _____ it already.
9. I (feel) _____ a bit tired. Can we go out tomorrow instead?

18 *My Family*

6. Transcript

I: Interviewer **T:** Tecwyn (8'08")

I: So, how, how many children have you got?
T: I have four.
I: Mhm, hmm.
T: I have er, a son who's um, hmm, how old's he now? He was born in '61. He's probably forty-three, a daughter who's forty-one, a daughter who's thirty-eight and a son who's thirty-seven.
I: Right. And are they all working?
T: And I, I just have one wife.
I: Right. (*laughs*) Is she Canadian?
T: No.
I: No.
T: No. She was born in er, England and er, she is er, her father was English, her mother was Irish. She spent **(1) the war years** in Ireland.
I: Mmm. How did you two meet up?
T: We worked together in London.
I: Oh, right. That was er, doing banking, wasn't it?
T: Yeah.
I: OK. Um, **(2) how did you get into banking?**
T: How did I get into banking?
I: Mmm.
T: Phew! That's sort of a long story, I guess. Um, I, I applied to work for an Eastern exchange bank . . .
I: Mmm.
T: . . . er, with the intention that I would go overseas again.
I: Right. What do you mean 'again'? Had you been before, then?
T: Well, I'd, I'd done a tour out in er, the Far East with the army.
I: Oh, right.
T: So . . . er, anyway **(3) I ended up being offered** a job to go to Canada, so I took it.
I: Right. Um, that must have been a, **(4) a big step** to go Canada.
T: Yep, yep, it was.
I: Right. Where did you end up first?
T: Well, I, I flew into Toronto, which was the head office of the bank, and then they . . . I was there for about two or three days, they sent me to Ottawa.
I: Mmm. Did you have a choice?
T: No, no. Er, I went to Ottawa for some training.
I: Mmm, right.
T: I was there for three years.
I: Mmm, hmm.
T: I was then transferred to Montreal.
I: Right.
T: I was there for two years. I was then transferred to Winnipeg.
I: Uh, huh.
T: I was there for four summers and five winters.
I: Right. (*laughs*) Is that significant, the five winters?

T: Yeah.
I: Why?
T: 'Cos **(5) it's bloody cold!**
I: (*laughs*) How cool does it get?
T: Well, I think there was er, one winter there where the temperature didn't come above 25 degrees below zero . . .
I: Right.
T: . . . for two weeks.
I: That is **(6) pretty cold**, yes.
T: It's cold.
I: Mmm. OK. And so then, after Winnipeg?
T: I was transferred to Vancouver . . .
I: Right.
T: . . . where I've been ever since.
I: OK. Um, of all the places you've been to in Canada, do you prefer Vancouver?
T: Absolutely.
I: Mmm. What's, what's so nice about it, 'cos I've never been?
T: Well, Vancouver is er . . . well, first of all it's the climate. The climate is very much as it is here in the UK.
I: Mmm.
T: Perhaps, on average, better.
I: Right.
T: And it's a beautiful part of the world. We've got, you know, mountains, forests, seaside – **(7) all that's good stuff**.
I: Mmm.
T: And we don't have those horrible winters that they have **(8) pretty well everywhere else in Canada**.
I: Right.
T: So the 'low mainland', as they call it, of British Columbia . . .
I: Mmm, hmm.
T: . . . is er, probably **(9) the choice spot** in Canada.
I: Did you have your children in Vancouver, or?
T: Two of them were born in Winnipeg; two were born in Vancouver.
I: Right, OK. Um, do all your children work?
T: Yes.
I: Yeah. What do they do? What does the oldest do?
T: My oldest boy er, works for er, **(10) a pulp**, er, **mill** . . .
I: Mmm.
T: . . . in McKenzie, in northern British Columbia.
I: Right.
T: And er, he also gets involved in all sorts of other stuff as well.
I: Like what?
T: Well, he's, he's er, er, let's see. He's a . . . **(11) he attends to the installation of satellite dishes** in that part of the world.
I: Oh, right.
T: And er, you know, so any . . . anything and everything in a

technical way he can handle that way because he was with the er, telephone company for a number of years.

I: I see. OK. But that's two quite different things, isn't it, working in **(12) the lumber mill** . . .

T: **(13) He can turn his hand to anything.**

I: Right. So you must be very proud of him.

T: Well, yes. He has four boys . . .

I: Gosh!

T: And his wife, like mine, never worked.

I: Right.

T: He takes care of everything.

I: Mmm, hmm. OK. How old are the um, grandchildren? Your . . . his four?

T: His?

I: Yeah.

T: His boys are 13, 12, 11 and nine.

I: Right. So one after the other, then? (*laughs*) OK. Um, who comes next?

T: I have a daughter, Catherine . . .

I: Mmm, hmm.

T: . . . who is **(14) a programme analyst.**

I: Oh, with computers, then?

T: Yeah.

I: Yeah.

T: She has her own little company . . .

I: Oh, right.

T: . . . and **(15) she,** er, **freelances**, you might say.

I: Mmm.

T: She lives in the United States.

I: So, do you see her often?

T: Oh, yes . . .

I: OK.

T: . . . about **(16) a 2½ hour run** from our place to her place.

I: Right.

T: She had the first grandchild um . . . he is, er, now 17.

I: Right.

T: And **(17) she was divorced and re-married** and now has two more boys. They are four and two and a half.

I: OK. Right. So, so far I think it's seven boys?

T: So far . . . no . . .

I: No.

T: That's one, two . . . oh, yeah, sorry, OK. Then I have a daughter who is er, unmarried.

I: Mmm.

T: She's a world traveller.

I: Is she?

T: Ask er, Jill'll tell you all about her.

I: Uh, huh. Where is she at the moment?

T: At the moment she um, she works for a company called er, hmm, **(18) Rocky Mountain Railroad.**

I: Mmm, hmm.

T: And er, then she works there from April till October.

I: Mmm, hmm.

T: And then generally from November until the following April she'll travel anywhere in the world. She's done it all.

I: How wonderful.

T: But er, this November she's, she has a job in Antarctica, so . . .

I: Gosh! What's she doing up there?

T: Down there.

I: Sorry! (*laughs*) What's she doing down there?

T: Well, there's a, there's an Australian company that operates this Russian **(19) icebreaker**, which is also **(20) a research ship** . . .

I: Right.

T: . . . and which carries about a hundred to 125 paying passengers.

I: Mmm, hmm.

T: She looks after those passengers and her job is titled 'hotel manager'.

I: Right. So are there similarities with her summer job, then? I, I suppose there are with customer care and . . .

T: I guess there would be similarities. She, she's sort of a people person, you know.

I: Mmm, hmm. Right. And then there's one more . . .

T: I have a son, my young son.

I: Mmm, hmm.

T: He is er, he is unmarried but lives with er, his er, girl . . .

I: Mmm.

T: . . . who . . . we call them **(21) common law wives**.

I: Right. How long have they been together?

T: Oh, they've been together about four years.

I: Uh, huh.

T: And they have one small boy who is, I think he's three.

I: Right.

T: So he's number eight.

I: Mmm, hmm.

T: No, he's actually number seven.

I: Seven.

T: Um, my er, my daughter's littlest fellow is number eight.

I: OK.

T: So there you go!

I: Well, thank you for that, yes! (*laughs*) Do you have um, any other family in Canada?

T: No.

I: No. So your family's back in Wales?

T: I have one sister.

I: Mmm, hmm.

T: And you've met her.

I: Oh, yes, that's it. (*laughs*) Is she older or younger than you?

T: She's younger than I am.

I: Mmm, hmm.

7. Words and Phrases

1. **the war years** – the Second World War years between 1939 and 1945
2. **How did you get into banking?** – What made you decide on a career in banking?
3. **I ended up being offered** – eventually I was offered
4. **a big step** – a major life change
5. **it's bloody cold!** – (impolite) it's very cold!
6. **pretty cold** – quite cold
7. **all that's good stuff** – those are all good things
8. **pretty well everywhere else in Canada** – nearly everywhere else in Canada
9. **the choice spot** – the best place to live
10. **a pulp mill** – a building with machinery which turns felled trees into a substance used to make paper
11. **He attends to the installation of satellite dishes.** – a long way of saying that he puts up and connects satellite dishes
12. **the lumber mill** – the building with machinery which processes felled trees
13. **He can turn his hand to anything.** – He is very good at lots of different practical things.
14. **a programme analyst** – a person who analyses and writes computer programmes
15. **she freelances** – she does work for other organisations, but this is on a contractual basis and not as an employee
16. **a 2½-hour run** – a 2½ hour drive, as in 'It's a beautiful day. Shall we go for a drive in the country?'
17. **she was divorced and then remarried** – her first marriage ended in divorce, but then she married someone else
18. **Rocky Mountain Railroad** – the name of a famous scenic railway in British Columbia
19. **icebreaker** – a ship which is reinforced at the front so that it can travel through icy water in order to keep sea lanes open
20. **a research ship** – a ship which is used by scientists who are trying to discover new facts or test hypotheses
21. **common law wives** – women not officially married, but living with their partners as wives

UNIT 2 Yasmin

1. Pre-Listening Comprehension

A Schema building

Yasmin was born in Pakistan, but she and her family came to live in the UK when she was four. She has a strong Huddersfield accent. How much do you know about Pakistan? Discuss the following statements with a partner and mark them True or False.

1. T F The capital of Pakistan is Karachi.
2. T F Pakistan stretches from the Himalayas to the Arabian Sea.
3. T F Pakistan shares borders with Afghanistan, China, India and Iran.
4. T F The modern state of Pakistan was founded in 1847.

My Family

B Discussion

Discuss the questions in small groups. Share your answers with the class.

1. Why do you think Yasmin's parents wanted to move to the UK from Pakistan?
2. Would you like to visit Pakistan? Why/Why not?

C Normalisation

🎧 21

This exercise is designed to help you get used to Yasmin's voice. Listen to the first part of the interview and answer the questions.

1. How did Yasmin travel from Seven Sisters to Walthamstow?
   a) by bus
   b) by car
   c) by Underground
2. Which two cities does Yasmin mention?

D Anticipating the next word (aural)

🎧 22 to 🎧 28

🎧 29 to 🎧 35

Listen to tracks 22–28. There is a word missing from the end of each excerpt. Try to guess the missing word and write it down. Then listen to tracks 29–35 to check your answers. How well did you guess?

1. _____
2. _____
3. _____
4. _____
5. _____
6. _____
7. _____

Karachi

UNIT 2: *Yasmin* 23

2. Listening Comprehension

A Gap-Fill
🎧 36

In this first exercise, Yasmin talks about her brothers and sisters. Before you listen, try to predict which words, or which types of words, will fit in the gaps. Then listen and check your answers.

1. Yasmin's parents have _____ girls and one boy.
2. Nasreen is the _____ child and Shazia is the _____.
3. Yasmin's _____ finds English names really _____ to pronounce.
4. The second oldest daughter's name is P-__-__-__-__-__-__.
5. Yasmin's brother's name is S__-__-__-__-__-__.
6. The youngest daughter's name comes from a _____.
7. Her name is S-__-__-__-__-__.

B True/False
🎧 37

Yasmin talks about why her parents moved to England. Listen and decide if each statement is True (T) or False (F). Remember to give reasons for your answers.

1. T F Yasmin came to England when she was a little girl.
2. T F Yasmin's parents moved to England from a big city in Pakistan.
3. T F Yasmin's father had three older and three younger brothers.
4. T F Yasmin's father began working on a farm at the age of 12.
5. T F In Pakistan it seems only the oldest brother inherits the family's land.

C Gap-Fill
🎧 38

Yasmin talks about her mother's feelings about moving to England. Before you listen, try to predict which words, or which types of words, will fit in the gaps. Then listen and check your answers.

1. Yasmin says a lot of British and _____ people in the _____ Ages left their countries because they wanted 'to see the _____ and taste the _____' of other parts of the world.
2. Yasmin's parents came to England to benefit from the _____ and to find _____.
3. Yasmin's _____ didn't want to come to Britain at first.
4. She had been _____ at _____ when she was at school.

My Family

5. However, she was not _____ to _____ the village to pursue an _____.
6. This is why she was passionate about her _____ being _____.
7. She felt her daughters would have more of an _____ in Britain.

D True/False

Yasmin talks some more about her parents moving to England. Listen and decide if each statement is True (T) or False (F). Remember to give reasons for your answers.

1. T F Yasmin thinks her parents were in their 20s when they left Pakistan.
2. T F Yasmin thinks her parents were very brave to come to England.
3. T F Yasmin says her parents are in their 60s now.
4. T F Yasmin remembers very cold winters in England as a child.
5. T F On one occasion a neighbour had to help Yasmin's mother open the door because the lock was frozen.

E Questions

Yasmin talks about an incident from her childhood. Listen and answer the questions.

1. Who brought home a mango one day, when Yasmin was eight or nine years old?
2. How much did each child get to taste?
3. Who went without?
4. What did Yasmin's parents keep in Pakistan?
5. When did Yasmin last visit Pakistan?
6. Where did Yasmin see masses of mango trees?
7. Which words does Yasmin use to describe the mangos?

3. Interesting Language Points

A The present simple

We often use the present simple to talk about facts and things that happen regularly. Look at these excerpts from Yasmin's interview:

> my mum <u>finds</u> English names difficult
> the name <u>doesn't</u> quite rhyme with the rest of us

B The simple past

We use the simple past to talk about completed actions in the past. We often use the simple past with a time expression, as in these examples from the interview:

> My parents <u>brought</u> me over when I was four.
> They <u>came</u> here to benefit from the economy and work.
> When she was at school she <u>was</u> brilliant at maths.
> I can remember when I was about eight or nine, my father <u>brought</u> one mango.
> I <u>went</u> there about six years ago.

C The past continuous

We use the past continuous to indicate that an action continued for a period of time in the past. We often use the simple past and the past continuous together when a longer action is interrupted by a shorter one, as in these examples:

> 'I was having a shower when you called, so that's why it went to voicemail.'

> 'Just to let you know Andreas is in hospital with a broken leg. Apparently he was painting the ceiling when his mobile rang and he fell off the ladder.'

Now look at these examples of the past continuous from the interview:

> *I think my father was reading a novel . . .* (i.e. at the time the youngest child was born)
> *My father was working . . .* (i.e. when he lived in Pakistan)
> *The lock was frozen in the door and she was trying to . . . struggling to open it . . .* (i.e. when a passer-by tried to help)
> *and I was thinking . . . it's nothing to have three or four mangoes in one day . . .* (i.e. while she was on holiday in Pakistan)

My Family

D The present perfect simple

We use the present perfect simple to talk about things we have done during a period of time leading up to the present, as in these examples from the interview. Remember that in spoken English *I have done* normally becomes *I've done*.

> I think over the years I've just developed a huge level of respect for my parents . . .
> I've only ever been to Pakistan once in my life . . .

E *would* when talking about the past

When talking about her father, Yasmin says:

> his feeling was that everybody would get a share of the land

In this case Yasmin is using *would* to make a prediction about the past – what was likely to happen if her father didn't leave Pakistan. Here are some more examples:

> 'When I was younger I was sure I would never own my own flat.'
> 'I was worried my car wouldn't start this morning as I haven't used it in weeks.'

Later in the interview Yasmin says:

> in the late 60s, there'd be [i.e. there would be] several feet of snow sometimes

In this case Yasmin is using *would* to talk about something that used to happen often. Here are some more examples of this usage:

> 'When we went to visit my grandmother, my brother and I would spend hours playing with her dog in the garden.'
> 'When I lived in Paris I would have a croissant for breakfast every morning.'

F *remember doing something* for reminiscing

We often use this structure when we talk about our childhoods. Look at these examples:

> 'I remember skating on this lake when I was 11.'
> 'Do you remember meeting me for the first time?'
> 'I remember waking up shivering every morning in winter until we got central heating.'

Now look at Yasmin's example:

> I remember thinking back to that childhood story.

4. Further Listening Practice

A Recognising sentence stress

🎧 41

Stressed words are the most important in spoken English because they carry the most meaning. Which words do you think Yasmin stresses in the following extracts?

1. I've got two older sisters, then myself, and my brother and then two younger sisters.
2. my mum finds English names difficult
3. they wanted to see the um, wealth and taste the fruit of other parts of the world
4. so her brothers could leave
5. Actually they were not so young . . .
6. Maybe my mum was in her mid-thirties. My, my dad might have been in his late thirties.
7. the winters used to be freezing
8. my father brought one mango
9. I've only ever been to Pakistan once in my life . . .
10. and I was thinking, you know, there people sort of have . . . it's nothing to have three or four mangoes in one day

Now listen to find out if your predictions were correct.

B Pronunciation – cup /ʌ/ and put /ʊ/

🎧 42

Like many native speakers in northern England and the Midlands, Yasmin does not distinguish the /ʌ/ vowel sound found in the word cup in standard English from the /ʊ/ vowel sound found in put.

Listen to how Yasmin pronounces the following words from the interview, and then listen to how your teacher pronounces them in standard English:

brother   youngest   young   succulent

Can you now imitate Yasmin's pronunciation, just for fun?

28 *My Family*

C Linking

When a word ends in a consonant in spoken English and the next word begins with a vowel, or when one word ends in the same letter as the letter at the start of the following word, the end of the first word will link with the start of the second word, making it sound as if the two words are one.

Listen to these excerpts and mark where linking occurs. Then check the answers with your teacher.

1. I've got two older sisters...
2. I think it's all to do with familiarity.
3. my mum finds English names difficult
4. he'd worked on the land
5. and taste the fruit of other parts of the world
6. because of the morality there, I suppose, pertaining to girls and women
7. I'll have to really work this out.
8. there'd be several feet of snow

D Recognising individual words in a stream of speech – Dictation

With a partner, listen and write the sentences or phrases you hear. Check your answers with the class.

1. _____
2. _____
3. _____
4. _____
5. _____
6. _____
7. _____
8. _____

UNIT 2: *Yasmin*

5. Further Language Development

A Gap-Fill

🎧 52

Try to predict the missing words before you listen.

I: Interviewer   **Y:** Yasmin

I: How did you **(1)** _____ here today?

Y: Oh, I came **(2)** _____ tube.

I: OK. Seven Sisters?

Y: That's **(3)** _____, yeah. So um, (coughs) Neil's ever so **(4)** _____, so he **(5)** _____ me the route from his home 'cos I'm not **(6)** _____ with the area. So **(7)** _____ night we **(8)** _____ a walk. 'Cos we'd been, I'd been **(9)** _____ in the car from, from Leeds and then to Birmingham, so (coughs) the idea was **(10)** _____ have a stretch and um, have a little walk and so he, he wanted to show me the route from his home. And I'm **(11)** _____ for getting **(12)** _____ (laughs) and getting **(13)** _____ with my left and my **(14)** _____!

I: Well, I'll take you **(15)** _____ to the tube so you know you're safe.

30   *My Family*

B Extension exercise

Fill in the blanks in these new sentences with words you heard during Yasmin's interview. The words are listed in the box to help you. One of the words is used twice.

> allowed   benefit   brilliant   climate   confused
> considerate   ever   find   getting   land   lock   work
> masses   motivation   notorious   novel   persuaded   rest
> rhymes   route   slice   stretch   struggling   used

1. How are you _____ home? Would you like a lift?
2. My best friend Claus is very _____. He always remembers my birthday.
3. What's the best _____ to your house from the motorway?
4. When you've been sitting in front of the computer for hours it's a good idea to stand up and have a _____.
5. My father is _____ for forgetting things. He even forgot my birthday!
6. Sorry, but I'm a bit _____. Please explain that again.
7. I _____ it very difficult to make time to relax. I tend to work too hard.
8. Have you come across a _____ by Nicholas Drayson called *Confessing a Murder*? It's one of the best books I've ever read.
9. I think you'll find the word 'kir' in French _____ with 'fear', not 'fir'.
10. Can you bring the _____ of the shopping in from the car for me?
11. Until the Industrial Revolution in England, people used to work on the _____, but then they started moving to the towns and cities.
12. A lot of people from Eastern Europe come to live in Britain to _____ from the higher wages here.
13. She's a really good actress, but she lacks _____ so she doesn't try hard enough to get work.
14. Ben didn't want to come to the party but I _____ him by telling him there'd be lots of food!
15. My neighbor's son is _____ at squash. He won the national under-15s championship last year.
16. When I was young we weren't _____ to have dessert until we'd eaten all our vegetables.

UNIT 2: *Yasmin*   31

17. I can't _____ out how old Kim is. Is she 11 or 12?
18. When we were kids, we _____ to play terrible games like ringing people's doorbells and running away.
19. My key broke in the _____ last night so I had to break a window to get in. Now I've got to find a locksmith who won't charge the earth.
20. I was _____ up the road with five bags of shopping yesterday afternoon when my neighbour stopped their car and offered me a lift. Wasn't that _____?
21. The _____ in New Zealand is similar to that of the UK, except the seasons are reversed.
22. Would you like another _____ of cake?
23. Have you _____ been to Seville? We're going there next week for a mini-break.
24. We've got _____ of tomatoes growing in the garden. Would you like to take some home?

C The simple past and the past continuous

Put the verbs in brackets into the appropriate tense.

1. I (*break*) _____ my elbow last August when I (*get*) _____ on a train and (*trip*) _____.
2. We (*go*) _____ to sell this house this time last year, but then we (*decide*) _____ to stay put.
3. Sorry I (*leave*) _____ the party without saying goodbye, but I (*have*) _____ to take Anneke home as she (*feel*) _____ ill.
4. I (*sit*) _____ in the garden yesterday reading a good book when suddenly the heavens (*open*) _____.
5. I (*plan*) _____ to go to university next year, but then I (*decide*) _____ to get more work experience first.
6. We (*drive*) _____ along quite happily when the car (*come*) _____ to a halt and I (*realise*) _____ that we'd run out of petrol.
7. I (*see*) _____ Carl while I (*stand*) _____ in the queue at the post office.
8. Dinner will be a bit late because I (*watch*) _____ a programme on telly and I (*forget*) _____ to put the oven on.

6. Transcript

I: Interviewer **Y:** Yasmin (6'19")

I: How did you get here today?
Y: Oh, I came by **(1) tube**.
I: OK. Seven Sisters?
Y: That's right, yeah. So um, (*coughs*) Neil's ever so **(2) considerate**, so he showed me the route from his home 'cos **(3) I'm not familiar with the area.** So last night we took a walk. 'Cos we'd been, I'd been sitting in the car from, from Leeds and then to Birmingham, so (*coughs*) the idea was we'd **(4) have a stretch** and um, have a little walk and so he, he wanted to show me the route from his home. And **(5) I'm notorious for getting lost** (*laughs*) and **(6) getting confused with my left and my right!**
I: Well, I'll take you back to the tube so you know you're safe. OK. Um, Yasmin, can you tell me about your family? Do you come from a big family?
Y: Er, yes, yeah. Quite, quite big, **(7) I suppose.** Um, I've got two older sisters, then myself, and my brother and then two younger sisters.
I: Right. Can you tell me their names?
Y: (*laughs*) Can I remember them?! (*laughs*). OK, Nasreen is the eldest, and then Perveen and then myself, Yasmin, and then my brother, Sarfraz, um, my younger sister, Shaheen, and then the youngest, Shazia.
I: OK. They're very difficult names, aren't they ... for an English person.
Y: Um, I think it's all to do with **(8) familiarity.** I mean, **(9) for instance** my mum finds English names difficult. (*laughs*) So I think, I think it's all to do with your, **(10) our standpoint** of what is difficult or not **(11) is dictated by** what is familiar and unfamiliar.
I: But take me through those names, like Shaheen. I think S-H-A-H-double E-N. Is that right?
Y: Yes. That's right, yes.
I: And yours is Y-A-S-M-I-N.
Y: That's right, yes.
I: OK. What about the other ones?
Y: Um, Nasreen. N-A-S-double R-E-N [sic]. Er, Perveen, P-E-R-V-double E-N. And er, then Sarfraz – S-A-R-F-R-A-Z. And then the youngest, Shazia. Er, I think my father was reading a novel (*laughs*) and **(12) the heroine's name** was Shazia, so her name doesn't quite **(13) rhyme** with the rest of us. (*laughs*) And so the youngest, her, hers S-H-A-Z-I-A.

I: OK. Were you born in this country?
Y: No, my parents brought me over when I was four.
I: From?
Y: Pakistan.
I: OK. Um, where in Pakistan?
Y: Er, near Lahore.
I: OK. Was it a village or a town?
Y: A village.
I: Why did they come to England?
Y: I think um, what my fa ... er, my father had six brothers – **(14) it sounds quite biblical, doesn't it!**) (*laughs*) And he was the eldest and um, and he'd worked on the land since he was 12. And the feeling was, his, his feeling was that um, **(15) everybody would get a share of the land** and, and so he just ... And the other ... So one aspect was the same reason that um, British, French people escaped in the Middle Ages and were exploring the rest of the planet because they wanted to (*coughs*) see the um, wealth and taste the fruit of other parts of the world.
I: Right.
Y: And so in a, **(16) in a similar fashion**, I think, um, he, they came here **(17) to um, benefit from the economy here** and, and work. So con . . . So my father was working. And um, my, my mother's **(18) motivation** was ... she was not happy with the idea of coming over at all, really. But then she was persuaded because when she was at school she was brilliant at maths but um, because of **(19) the morality** there, I suppose, **(20) pertaining to** girls and women, she was not allowed to leave the village **(21) to pursue** her education. So her brothers could leave and um, go to the town, but she wasn't allowed to. So she always felt this as a loss and so **(22) she was quite passionate about** her daughters being educated, and so that was her feeling – that in England her daughters would have that opportunity.
I: How old were your mum and dad when they came to England?
Y: Goodness me! Um ... (*laughs*) Actually they were not so young, I don't think. I'll have to, I'll have to really work this out. I'm not really sure. Maybe my mum was in her mid-30s.
I: Oh?
Y: My, my dad might have been in his late 30s.
I: Right. That, that is a big life change.

UNIT 2: *Yasmin* 33

Y: Yes, yes. I mean I think over the years I've just developed **(23) a huge level of** respect for my parents because I think they were so **(24) courageous** in er, in um, making this huge change um, and I can remember in the late 60s the winters used to be freezing and um, we'd be... there'd be several **(25) feet** of snow sometimes. And I can remember as a child my mum couldn't open the... **(26) the lock** was frozen in the door and she was trying to... **(27) struggling to open it** and **(28) a passer-by** tried to help as well. So they had... So this was the climate here, and, and they came from Pakistan which was the opposite climate.

Y: But also just things like as we, **(29) we get habituated to certain things** and you start to love certain fruits or certain food is natural to have. And, and er, I can remember when I was about eight or nine, my father brought one mango (*laughs*) and I can remember, you know, we all had a slice each and my mum didn't have one because she wanted us all to have more. And then (*coughs*) er, I've only ever been to Pakistan once in my life and my parents kept the farm and when I went there, which was about six years ago, (*coughs*) and um, the, the, the farm's **(30) an orchard** and they've got **(31) masses of** mango trees and, and I was thinking, you know, there people sort of have... it's nothing to have three or four mangoes in one day and, and they're so **(32) succulent** and fresh and, and, and I, and I remember thinking back to that childhood memory.

I: That's, that's a really nice story.

7. Words and Phrases

1. **tube** – the London Underground
2. **considerate** – thoughtful and kind
3. **I'm not familiar with the area** – I don't know the area very well
4. **have a stretch** – to straighten your body after a long period of being in the same position, for example sitting in a car or in front of a computer
5. **I'm notorious for getting lost** – I'm famous for losing my way
6. **getting confused with my left and my right** – mixing up my left and right
7. **I suppose** – I guess that's true
8. **familiarity** – how well you know something
9. **for instance** – for example
10. **our standpoint** – your position in the world
11. **is dictated by** – is influenced by
12. **the heroine's name** – the name of the main female character in a novel
13. **rhyme** – words which rhyme have a similar sound, e.g. house/mouse, lice/mice
14. **it sounds quite biblical** – it sounds like something out of the Bible
15. **everybody would get a share of the land** – they would divide the land between the brothers
16. **in a similar fashion** – in the same way
17. **to benefit from the economy here** – to enjoy the economic advantages of living in Britain
18. **motivation** – your personal reason for doing something
19. **the morality there** – the standards that dictate people's behaviour
20. **pertaining to** – concerning
21. **to pursue** – to continue
22. **she was quite passionate about** – she felt quite strongly about it
23. **a huge level of** – a large amount of
24. **courageous** – brave
25. **feet** – (plural of foot) There are 12 inches in one foot. One inch is 2.54 centimetres.
26. **the lock** – the device in a door that you need a key to open
27. **struggling to open it** – trying very hard to open the door
28. **a passer-by** – somebody walking past the house
29. **we get habituated to certain things** – we get used to particular things
30. **an orchard** – an area of land where non-citrus fruit trees are grown
31. **masses of** – loads of, lots of
32. **succulent** – pleasantly juicy

UNIT 2: *Yasmin*

UNIT 3 Scott

1. Pre-Listening Comprehension

A Schema building

Scott is a young man from Australia who lives in the UK. How much do you know about Australia? Discuss the following statements with a partner and mark them True or False.

1. T F People from overseas make up one quarter of the population of Australia.
2. T F The capital of Australia is Sydney.
3. T F Australia is the third-biggest country in the world.

My Family

B Discussion

Discuss the questions in small groups. Share your answers with the class.

1. What else do you know about Australia?
2. How many adjectives can you come up with to describe Australia?
3. Would you like to live in Australia? Why/Why not?
4. Do you know what an Australian accent sounds like?

C Normalisation

🎧 54 to 🎧 58
🎧 59 to 🎧 63

This exercise is designed to help you get used to Scott's voice. Listen to tracks 54–58. There is a word missing from the end of each excerpt. Try to guess the missing word and write it down. Then listen to tracks 59–63 to check your answers. How well did you guess?

1. _____
2. _____
3. _____
4. _____
5. _____

UNIT 3: *Scott*

2. Listening Comprehension

A Questions
🎧 64

In this first exercise, Scott talks about his immediate family. Listen and answer the questions.

1. Scott is 23 years old. How old is his sister?
2. What does Scott's brother work as?
3. Is Scott's brother a homeowner?
4. How far does Scott's sister live from Scott's brother?
5. What did Scott's sister do before the two brothers?
6. How old are Scott's mum and dad at the moment?
7. What had Scott's parents never done until last year?
8. Who does Scott call regularly?

B True/False
🎧 65

Scott talks about his grandparents, who were still around when he was growing up. Listen and decide if each statement is True (T) or False (F). Remember to give reasons for your answers.

1. T F His maternal grandfather's name doesn't sound very Scottish.
2. T F Scott's maternal grandfather was born and grew up in Scotland.
3. T F Scott's paternal grandfather came to Australia from England when he was a teenager.
4. T F Only one of Scott's grandparents was born in England.
5. T F Australian citizens don't need a visa to live and work in the UK.
6. T F Scott's grandparents always used to make the children eat healthily.
7. T F Scott's grandparents had their children quite late in life.
8. T F Scott's grandparents all died within 10 years of each other.
9. T F Scott is pleased that none of his grandparents had to spend years on their own.

38 *My Family*

3. Interesting Language Points

A **The present simple and the present continuous**

We generally use the present simple to talk about facts and things that happen regularly. Look at these excerpts from Scott's interview:

> I <u>come</u> from a family of five.
> She <u>lives</u> about a kilometre the other way from my parents.
> I <u>try</u> to get on the phone to mum as often as I can because I <u>know</u> she <u>appreciates</u> it and <u>does miss</u> me.
> So that <u>makes</u> me second-generation Australian.

We generally use the present continuous to talk about things that are happening at the moment. Look at these excerpts from Scott's interview:

> She<u>'s</u> also <u>expecting</u> her first child at the moment.
> They<u>'re</u> still very much <u>living</u> off that.

Now look at this sentence from the interview which includes both the present simple and the present continuous:

> they <u>are living</u> the typical life that most people in that area <u>live</u>

The meaning here is that his brother and sister have lived in other places, but they are currently living the kind of life that is typical for a lot of people in Australia.

B **The simple past and the present perfect simple**

We use the simple past to talk about completed actions in the past. We often use the simple past with a time expression, as in these examples from the interview:

> they <u>had</u> their first overseas trip last year
> My dad's father <u>moved</u> to Australia when he <u>was</u> about 15.
> They <u>passed away</u> maybe 10 years ago.

We use the present perfect simple to talk about things that have happened during a period of time leading up to the present:

> 'He <u>has travelled</u> a little bit' (i.e. in his life up until now)
> 'he<u>'s ended up</u> back there and <u>bought</u> his own house'
> 'they<u>'ve</u> both pretty much <u>stayed</u> in the area'
> 'I<u>'ve been</u> the one to move away overseas'

C *because* → *'cos* in spoken English

In fast spoken English *because* is often shortened to *'cos*, as in these examples from the interview:

> *I'm lucky that my grandparent was born in England 'cos that, that's allowed me to get the ancestral visa to stay here.*

> *And they all passed away within about four or five years of each other which um, in a way was, was really good 'cos you can see that um, when one's left for a long time they can tend to get quite lonely . . .*

4. Further Listening Practice

A Recognising sentence stress

Stressed words are the most important in spoken English because they carry the most meaning. Which words do you think Scott stresses in the following extracts?

1. *I come from a family of five . . .*
2. *so three children and I'm the middle child*
3. *so I've got an older brother and a younger sister*
4. *and a mother and a father who are still both alive*
5. *Also my sister, obviously the youngest, but the first to get married.*
6. *And my parents are both sort of um, approaching 60 now.*
7. *and I'm lucky that my grandparent was born in England*
8. *I guess they had their children reasonably late for their um, generation*
9. *my parents certainly had us quite late for their generation*

Now listen to find out if your predictions were correct.

B Recognising individual words in a stream of speech – Dictation

With a partner, listen and write the sentences or phrases you hear. Check your answers with the class.

1. _____
2. _____
3. _____
4. _____

UNIT 3: *Scott* 41

C Rising and falling intonation

🎧 71

Traditionally students are taught that the speaker's voice falls at the end of statements and this is, indeed, the case with many British native speakers of English. However, many younger British native speakers and native speakers from Australia and New Zealand tend to have a rising intonation pattern at the end of statements.

Listen and mark with arrows (↗ ↘) whether you hear a rise or fall at the end of each statement:

1. *I come from a family of five...*
2. *and a younger sister*
3. *and my parents are both sort of um, approaching 60 now*
4. *And they had their first overseas trip last year.*
5. *all my grandparents are now deceased*
6. *certainly as a child I had four grandparents*

5. Further Language Development

A Extension exercise

Fill in the blanks in these new sentences with words you heard during Scott's interview. The words are listed in the box to help you.

> appreciates   effort   ended up   expecting   grateful
> great   grew up   lonely   lucky   middle   miss
> on   passed away   side   travel agent   visa

1. I don't like it when my brother and his wife argue because I always get caught in the _____.
2. You have to put in a lot of _____ to learn a language.
3. One of the perks of being a _____ is that you get a discount on flights and package trips.
4. I was born in Ankara, but I _____ in Istanbul.
5. We _____ not getting home till gone midnight.
6. Mia is leaving work in September because she's _____ a baby.
7. We're really _____ to you for letting us stay with you and it was _____ to see you both again.
8. I'm sorry, she's _____ the phone. Can she call you back?
9. My grandfather really _____ you doing his shopping now he can't drive any more.
10. I love living in New York, but I do _____ my family and friends back in Britain.
11. I'm usually really _____ at cards.
12. I think you need a _____ to work in the USA.
13. My grandfather on my mother's _____ unfortunately _____ before I was born.
14. London can be a very _____ place, even though you're always surrounded by loads of people.

UNIT 3: Scott

B **The present simple and continuous, the simple past and the present perfect simple**

Put the verbs in brackets into the appropriate tense.

1. Have you got any aspirin? I think I (*get*) _____ a headache.
2. This is the third time I (*have*) _____ French fries this week!
3. I always (*sing*) _____ when I'm in the shower.
4. Paul (*stay*) _____ at our place last night.
5. Robert (*walk*) _____ from Land's End to John O'Groats this coming summer to raise money for charity.
6. Generally I (*read*) _____ when I'm on a train, but I was so tired last time I (*take*) _____ one that I (*fall*) _____ asleep even before the train had left the station.
7. I (*get*) _____ really fed up with work. I (*think*) _____ it's time I (*got*) _____ another job.
8. We (*not see*) _____ Simon since he (*go*) _____ to work in Spain. Is he still there, do you know?
9. Paul (*give up*) _____ smoking at last. I'm really proud of him. I never (*think*) _____ he'd do it.
10. We (*have*) _____ a party next Saturday. Can you make it? It (*be*) _____ ages since we last (*meet*) _____.

C **Transformations**

Change the word in each bracket which Scott used in his interview to form a word which fills the gap.

1. Don't forget – I shall be following your progress _____. (*close*)
2. He's not a difficult child, but he is very _____. I don't know where he gets his energy! (*alive*)
3. A lot of younger people in Britain think _____ is a bit old-fashioned these days. (*married*)
4. The 19th century saw the _____ of the middle classes in Europe. (*grew*)
5. I don't like _____. I prefer to stay at home. (*travelled*)
6. Can't you work it out? The answer's _____. (*obviously*)
7. This road's so _____. I wish they'd fill in all the potholes. (*bump*)
8. I love this time of year when the leaves start _____ red and yellow. (*turns*)

44   *My Family*

9. We're trying to eat more _____ these days, so we have lots of salads and fresh fruit and vegetables. (*health*)
10. My brother's studying _____ at art school. (*photos*)
11. My grandmother always took great _____ in her appearance. (*proudly*)
12. _____ you already! (*miss*)
13. In Germany universities students show their _____ of a good lecture by banging the tables with their knuckles. (*appreciates*)
14. Thank you very much for all your _____ over the past few weeks. (*supporting*)
15. This is the _____ spot where I tripped. You can see how uneven the sidewalk is. (*actually*)
16. James was very _____ as a child because he was the only boy with four elder sisters. (*spoiling*)
17. What is the _____ of the Latin saying 'Carpe diem'? (*mean*)
18. We _____ you'd be hungry when you got home so we ordered a pizza. (*guess*)
19. The asking price is £250,000, but that's quite _____ for a house in this area. (*reasonably*)
20. Wishing you good health and _____ in the coming year. (*happy*)

UNIT 3: *Scott*

6. Transcript

I: Interviewer **S:** Scott (3'35")

I: Can you tell me about your family, please?
S: Yes, OK. Well, I come from a family of five, um, so three children and I'm the middle child. Um, we're all pretty close together, about two years in-between each child, so I've got an older brother and a younger sister. Er, and a mother and a father who are still both alive and both er, married, which is **(1) a good, good effort** these days, I think. Um, and my older brother is **(2) a travel agent** living pretty much half a kilometre from where my parents live er, in Croydon back home, where he was born and grew up. He has travelled a little bit, but **(3) he's ended up**, ended up back there and bought his own house. And my sister, who's the youngest of the family, was the first one to marry. Um, and she lives about a kilometre the other way from my parents, so they've both very much um, stayed in the area and are living the, the typical life that, that most people in that area live, whereas I've been the one to move away **(4) overseas**. Also my sister, obviously the youngest, but the first to get married, and she's also expecting her first child at the moment, so she's starting to get **(5) a little bump**, I believe.
I: Right.
S: And my parents are both sort of um, **(6) approaching** 60 now. My mum turns 60 this year. Um, **(7) both in pretty good health**, which I'm **(8) grateful for**. And they had their first overseas trip last year. They, they came over to visit me in London, which for them was **(9) a trip of a lifetime** and they're still very much um, **(10) living off that** and **(11) showing the photos off** very proudly to friends and family. So that was **(12) great** to see them over here and um . . . Yeah. I, I try to get on the phone to mum as often as I can because I know **(13) she appreciates it (14) and does miss me**, but um, **(15) they've been very good in supporting me and um, you know**.
I: That's great. Um, have you got any grandparents?
S: Er, all my grandparents **(16) are now deceased**, but er, certainly as a child I had four grandparents. Um, mum's side of the family were . . . well, her dad was from, was from a Scottish background, so his name was Fergus McAlpin, and it doesn't get much more Scottish than that. But they were both . . . certainly both my mother's parents were born in Australia. My dad's parents were from an English background um, and my dad's father was actually born in England. He moved to Australia when he was about 15. So that makes me **(17) second generation Australian**, which is about as far back as most people can go. Um, and I'm **(18) lucky** that my grandparent was born in England 'cos that, that's allowed me to get **(19) the ancestral visa to stay here**. But yeah, they were typical grandparents. Um, white hair and er, **(20) spoiling their grandchildren** and taking them to McDonald's at any opportunity. Er, but they all sort of . . . I guess they had their children **(21) reasonably late (22) for their um, generation,** and my parents certainly had us quite late for their generation. They were over 30 when they had children, which meant my grandparents were quite old, so they passed away maybe 10 years ago. And **(23) they all passed away** within about four or five years of each other which um, in a way was, was really good 'cos you can see that um, when one's left for a long time **(24) they can tend to get quite lonely**, so it wasn't such a bad thing to see them um, all go off very happy and after a good life.

My Family

7. Words and Phrases

1. a good **eff**ort these days – he thinks his parents have done well to stay married for so long when so many marriages end in divorce nowadays
2. a **tr**avel agent – someone whose job involves organising tickets, hotel rooms, etc. for customers who want to travel
3. he's ended up back there – now he's back there again
4. **over**seas – abroad (only when the country you are talking about is separated by water from another country you are talking about)
5. a little bump – her stomach has grown a little bigger because of the baby
6. app**ro**aching – nearing, coming up to
7. both in pretty good health – they are physically quite well
8. **gr**ateful for – thankful for
9. a trip of a **life**time – a very special holiday
10. living off that – the memory is still very much with them
11. showing the **ph**otos off – they are showing everyone their photos because they want people to see what a good time they had
12. great – really good, wonderful
13. she app**re**ciates it – it's important to her because it gives her pleasure
14. and does miss me – she feels a bit sad because her son is so far away
15. they've been very good in sup**por**ting me – they have helped him emotionally/financially
16. are now dec**ea**sed – (formal English) are now dead
17. second generation Aus**tr**alian – someone whose parents were born in Australia, but whose grandparent/s was/were born in another country
18. lucky – fortunate
19. the an**ce**stral **vi**sa to stay here – a visa which is given to the descendants of people whose grandparents (or at least one of them) were born in the UK
20. spoiling their **gr**andchildren – being very kind and generous to their grandchildren by giving them things they want and letting them do what they want
21. rea**so**nably late – quite late
22. for their generation – for people of around their age
23. they all passed away – a softer way of saying 'they died'
24. they can tend to get quite **lo**nely – they can become sad because they don't have anyone to talk to and they miss their partner/husband/wife

UNIT 3: *Scott*

UNIT 4 Carol

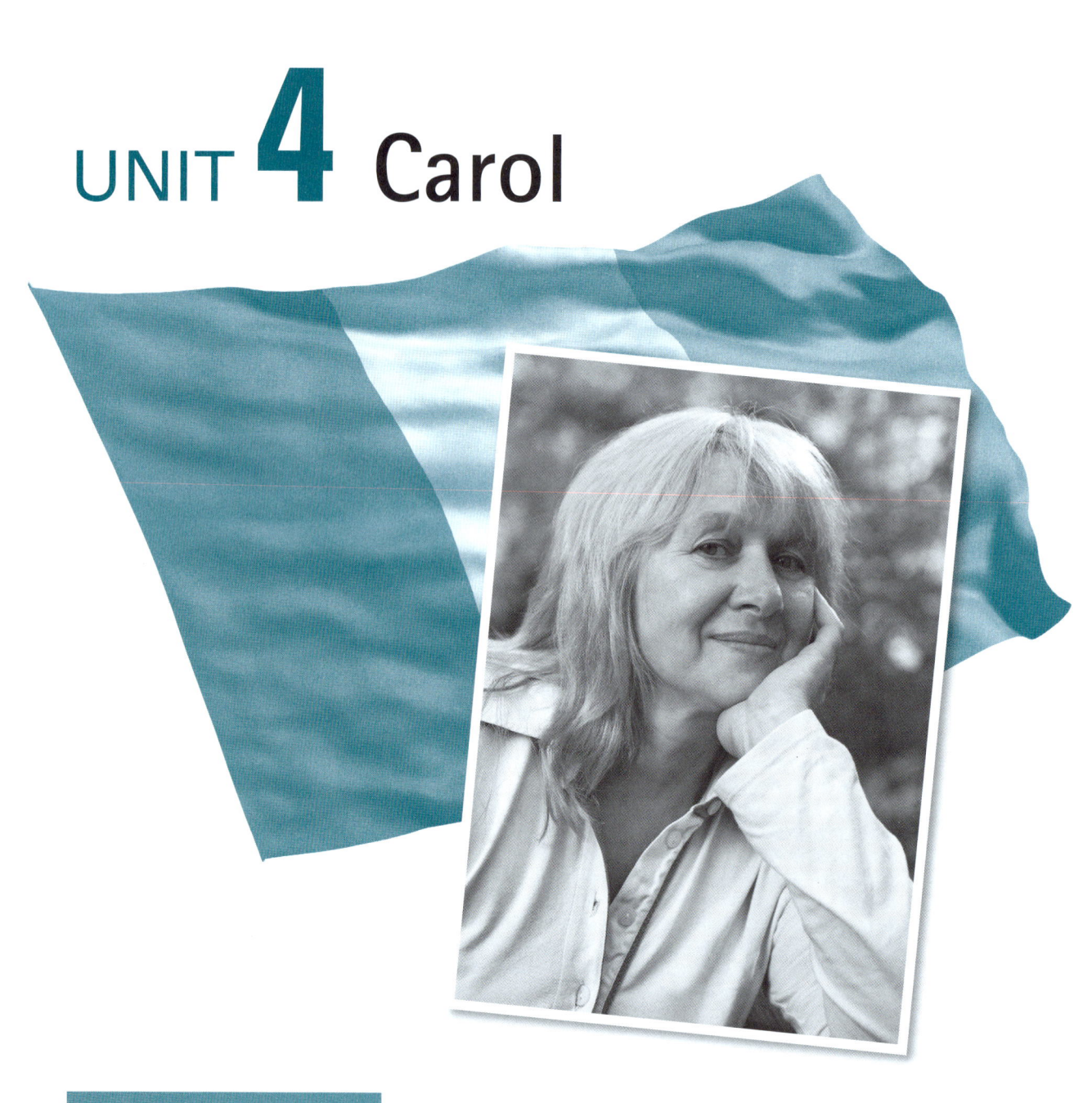

1. Pre-Listening Comprehension

A Schema building

Carol comes from Dublin, the capital of the Republic of Ireland, which is also known as Eire. How much do you know about the Republic of Ireland? Discuss the following statements with a partner and mark them True or False.

1. T F The currency of the Republic of Ireland is the Irish pound, or punt.
2. T F The capital of the Republic of Ireland is Dublin.
3. T F The patron saint of the Republic of Ireland is St. Paul.

B Discussion

Discuss the questions in small groups. Share your answers with the class.

1. What else do you know about the Republic of Ireland?
2. Give possible reasons why Carol decided to move to London.
3. Do you know what an Irish accent sounds like?

2. Listening Comprehension

A True/False

In this first exercise, Carol talks about her family back in Ireland. Listen and decide if each statement is True (T) or False (F). Remember to give reasons for your answers.

1. T F Carol has five brothers and sisters.
2. T F Despite living in England for 10 years, Carol still calls Ireland 'home'.
3. T F Carol grew up in a village just outside Dublin.
4. T F Carol's brothers and sisters and her parents lived in a huge house.
5. T F Carol jokes that she and her brothers and sisters were too poor to sleep in beds.
6. T F Carol was 44 years old at the time of the interview.
7. T F Carol has a good relationship with her sister in England.
8. T F Carol hardly ever goes back to Ireland.

B Questions

Carol talks about her children and her partner. Listen and answer the questions.

1. What are the names of Kim's brothers?
2. What did Kim finish in May?
3. Who does Kim like?
4. What does she never feel in her new career?
5. Does she earn more money now than in her last job?
6. Where did Kim work before she began her new career?
7. Who works in the same place as Kim used to?
8. Which part of Carol's partner's body does she describe as 'nice'?
9. What is her partner's job?

3. Features of an Irish accent

A **The glottal stop**

🎧 75

The glottal stop (i.e. not pronouncing fully the *–t* sound at the end of words such as *got* or *lot*, or the *–t–* sounds in words such as *bottle* or *kettle*) is a common feature of many British accents, and is used particularly by younger people.

Underline, note down or call out where Carol uses a glottal stop in the following excerpts:

> *I've got a sister here. I've got a brother here.*
> *two sisters at home and a brother at home*
> *but it was Dublin*
> *as little as possible*
> *She absolutely loves it.*

B *doing → doin'*

🎧 76

Irish speakers of English often leave the final letter *g* off the ends of words, as in the following examples:

> *She likes not knowin' what's coming next.*
> *She's doin' somethin' all the time.*

Can you hear the difference when your teacher says these sentences?

C **Pronunciation – *cup* /ʌ/ and *put* /ʊ/**

🎧 77

As we heard in Yasmin's interview, many native English speakers in areas such as northern England, the Midlands and the Irish Republic do not distinguish the /ʌ/ vowel sound found in the word *cup* in standard English from the /ʊ/ vowel sound found in *put*.

Listen to how Carol, and then your teacher, pronounce the following excerpts from the interview:

> *and me mother's here*
> *I come in the middle somewhere.*
> *The youngest is . . . 29.*
> *five months*
> *She absolutely loves it.*
> *He's the manager of the pub I work in.*

50   *My Family*

D *and* → *an'*, *my* → *me*, *th* → *t*

🎧 78 to 🎧 80

Carol and other Irish speakers of English often drop the final letter *-d* from the word *and*, as in this example:

> *Two sisters at home an' a brother at home.*

They also often change *my* to *me*:

> *And me mother's here.*

Finally, the *th* sound found in words such as *three* or *think* is often pronounced as *t*, resulting in *tree* and *tink*. Listen to how Carol pronounces *teeth* in the following excerpt:

> *he has nice teeth*

4. Further Language Development

A Extension exercise Fill in the blanks in these new sentences with words you heard during Carol's interview. The words are listed in the box to help you.

> about   bored   centre   drawer   get
> grew   handy   home   laid   moody
> paid   still   training   used

1. I _____ up in Southampton, but I moved to London when I was 18.
2. We live five minutes from the station, so it's very _____ for getting to work.
3. It's impossible to drive into the city _____ on Saturdays because the traffic's so bad.
4. I'm lucky because I _____ on well with everyone I work with.
5. What time did you get _____ on Friday?
6. I was _____ £8 an hour in my last job, but I get £10 an hour here.
7. Pavel is very _____ back. He never gets stressed about anything.
8. I can't open this _____. It seems to be stuck.
9. My cousin is _____ to become a journalist.
10. I'm _____ at work. I'll call you when I'm leaving.
11. We _____ to go fishing here when I was a kid.
12. Tell me _____ your holiday. Anders said you'd been to Seville. I bet it was fantastic, wasn't it?
13. I'm so _____. Can't we go out or something?
14. I find Pierre very _____. Sometimes he's really friendly and you can have a nice chat and then the next day he won't even say hello.

My Family

B Prepositions and adverbs

Choose which preposition or adverb in the box fits each gap in these sentences based on Carol's interview. Some of them are used more than once.

> about   as   at   for   in   like
> long   of   often   on   out   over
> since   to   until   up   well   with

1. What's your book _____?
2. Have you heard what happened _____ Tim on holiday?
3. I'm going to stay _____ tonight. I'm too tired to go _____.
4. Sorry, I left my homework _____ home.
5. There's a fantastic Thai restaurant _____ the city centre, so we could go there if you like.
6. Why don't you come _____ here and sit _____ us?
7. I'm very lucky because I get _____ _____ with my wife's parents.
8. How _____ did you spend in Sweden?
9. I don't _____ go out during the week because I have to get _____ early to go _____ work.
10. What does your girlfriend work _____?
11. I haven't seen Paul _____ he started going out _____ Susanna.
12. I'm getting bored _____ work. I think it's time I looked _____ another job.
13. The Government is trying to encourage students to stay _____ school _____ they're 18.
14. I'm not used _____ going so fast. Could you slow down a bit, please?
15. Doesn't Sarah look _____ her mother?
16. David's mum is the manager _____ the gym I used to go _____.

UNIT 4: Carol

5. Transcript

I: Interviewer   **C:** Carol   (3'23")

I: Can you tell me about your family, 'cos your mum's still alive …
C: Yeah.
I: … and you've got brothers and sisters, I think.
C: I've got a sister here, I've got a brother here and me mother's here.
I: Right. What about the ones in Ireland?
C: Two sisters at home and a brother at home.
I: So you still call Ireland home?
C: Oh yeah. Always will be, always will be.
I: Did you grow up in Dublin itself?
C: Yes. **(1) Born and reared.**
I: In the centre of the city?
C: Just outside the city centre, but it was Dublin.
I: What, what was that like? Lots of shops?
C: It was a, it was er, **(2) a housing scheme** type thing.
I: So was it a house you lived in?
C: A house, yeah. Two bedroomed house.
I: Um, how many children?
C: Six!
I: Six children! (*laughs*)
C: Yeah. We slept in a drawer. (*laughs*)
I: (*laughs*) OK. Are you the oldest?
C: Middle. I come in the middle somewhere, yeah.
I: OK. So how old is the oldest brother or sister now?
C: Oldest sister is … 54.
I: That's quite a bit older than you.
C: Yeah. Well … 10 years.
I: And the youngest?
C: **The youngest is … 29.**
I: Now you've got one sister over here?
C: One over here, yeah.
I: **(3) Do you get on very well with her?**
C: No! No, not at all.
I: How often do you see her?
C: I don't! (*laughs*) As little as possible. (*laughs*)
I: How often do you go back to Ireland?
C: Probably twice a year.
I: Mmm.
C: Mmm.
I: All right. Now, you've got three children.
C: Mmm, hmm.
I: Thomas, Kim and …
C: James.
I: James. Er, is Kim the oldest?
C: Yeah.
I: What does er, Kim work as?
C: Kim is a police officer.
I: Goodness me. How long has she been a police officer?
C: Since May.
I: May?
C: Yeah. She finished her training in May.
I: Right. How long did her training take?
C: Five months.
I: OK. Does she enjoy it?
C: **(4) She absolutely loves it.** She …
I: What does she like about it?
C: She likes … she likes not knowing what's coming next. She likes the adrenalin rush. She likes the people she works with. She's doing something all the time. She's not … She doesn't get time to get bored. Yeah, she loves it.
I: Does it pay well?
C: Better than what she was paid in her last job.
I: What was that?
C: That was in **(5) the law courts.**
I: OK. And Thomas, what does he do?
C: Thomas is still at school.
I: OK. And James?
C: James is in the law courts.
I: Where Kim used to be?
C: Where Kim used to be.
I: I see. OK. Um, and you've got a partner now?
C: Yeah.
I: Can you describe him to me, please?
C: Do I have to? (*laughs*) Well, today he's a **(6) moody (7) bastard.**
I: Right.
C: (*laughs*)
I: Generally …
C: Normally … yeah, but generally … he's a nice **(8) guy. (9) Laid back.**
I: How old is he?
C: Sixty.
I: Sixty. OK.
C: **(10) My sugar daddy.**
I: (*laughs*) Um, what does he look like?
C: What's he look like?
I: Is he … Is he tall?
C: Grey-haired, **(11) tallish. (12) Big build-ish.** Erm, he has nice teeth.
I: Nice teeth?
C: Yeah. (*laughs*)
I: Um, what does he work as?
C: He's the manager of the pub I work in.
I: Oh, that's quite **(13) handy, isn't it?**
C: Yeah.
I: OK.

My Family

6. Words and Phrases

1. **Born and reared.** – Born and brought up.
2. **a hous**ing **scheme** – subsidised housing provided by the authorities for people on benefits or low incomes
3. **Do you get on very well with her?** – Do you have a good relationship with her?
4. **She abso**lutely **loves it.** – Here 'absolutely' is used to strengthen the word 'loves'. Here are some more examples:
   I absolutely hate getting my feet wet.
   We were absolutely exhausted when we got home.
   That was an absolutely fantastic dinner! Thanks very much.
   There is absolutely nothing to eat in this fridge!
5. **the law courts** – the buildings and rooms where legal cases are heard
6. **moo**dy – When someone's mood is very changeable – sometimes they're cheerful and sometimes they're depressed. You never know what mood they are going to be in.
7. **ba**stard – (impolite) a word used to describe a person you are angry with. (The original definition is a person whose parents are not married.)
8. **guy** – an informal word for a man
9. **laid-back** – relaxed, not easily stressed
10. **My sugar dadd**y. – an expression used to describe a man who is having a relationship with a much younger woman
11. **tall**ish – quite tall
12. **big build-ish.** – Someone who is tall and muscular. –ish is added to indicate that he is fairly tall and muscular.
13. **hand**y – convenient

UNIT 4: *Carol*

UNIT 5 Barbara

1. Pre-Listening Comprehension

A Schema building

Barbara was born and brought up in Paderborn, in northern Germany. How much do you know about Germany? Circle the correct answer.

1. T F Germany is the largest European Union member state in terms of population.
2. T F Germany shares borders with four other European countries.
3. T F Germany has the largest economy in Europe.
4. T F Germany does not have any beaches.

B Discussion

Discuss the questions in small groups. Share your answers with the class.

1. What else do you know about Germany?
2. Why do you think Barbara speaks fluent Spanish, even though she has never studied it?
3. Do you know what a German accent sounds like?

2. Listening Comprehension

A Questions
(Track 82)

In this first exercise, Barbara gives some personal information. Listen and answer the questions.

1. Can you spell Barbara's surname?
2. What is the name of her street?
3. What is the postcode/zipcode?
4. What is Barbara's home telephone number?

B Gap-Fill
(Track 83)

Barbara talks about her husband and children. Before you listen, try to predict which words, or which types of words will fit in the gaps. Then listen and check your answers.

1. Barbara's _____ comes from _____.
2. Barbara's two sons are _____ and _____ years old.
3. Barbara says her sons are very _____.
4. They love _____ with _____.
5. Barbara's husband _____ in computing which is why they have _____ computers at home.
6. She has never played _____ on a computer.

C True/False
(Track 84)

Barbara talks about her husband, parents and brother. Listen and decide if each statement is True (T) or False (F). Remember to give reasons for your answers.

1. T F Barbara's husband came to Germany on a scholarship to study.
2. T F Barbara and Miguel will celebrate their silver wedding anniversary in two years' time.
3. T F Barbara's parents live in a house not far from Barbara and her family.
4. T F Barbara's brother is a priest in a church.
5. T F Barbara's brother also writes novels.

3. Features of a German accent

A **The final d of words pronounced as t**

🎧 85

In German if a word ends in *d*, this final *d* is pronounced *t*. Listen to how Barbara pronounces the following words and then listen to your teacher say them:

Well, I'm marrie<u>d</u>, and my husban<u>d</u>, he comes from Chile.

B **Pronunciation – *th***

🎧 86 to 🎧 87

A lot of non-native speakers find the *th* sound in words such as *with* and *the* difficult to pronounce. Often they use *s* or *z* instead. Listen to how Barbara pronounces the following words containing *th*, and then listen to your teacher say them:

but at <u>th</u>e moment they
in his part of <u>th</u>e world, yes

C ***v* and *f***

🎧 88

In German the letter *v* is pronounced as *f* and Barbara makes just one error when she pronounces *never* as *nefer* in the following extract:

No, ne<u>v</u>er.

D ***ch* and *sh***

🎧 89

In German the letters *ch* at the start of a word are pronounced *sh*. Listen to how Barbara says shance rather than chance in the following extract:

and just by <u>ch</u>ance we met

58 *My Family*

4. Further Language Development

A Extension exercise

Fill in the blanks in these new sentences with words you heard during Barbara's interview. The words are listed in the box to help you.

> accountant   chance   comes   famous   flat
> honest   lively   married   moment   professional
> quite   retired   romantic   silver   spell   works

1. My husband _____ from Pakistan.
2. I've got _____ a lot of cake left. Would you like to take some home?
3. We are celebrating our _____ wedding anniversary next year. Honestly, after 25 years with James I think I deserve a medal!
4. My wife _____ in banking and I'm self-employed.
5. The reason I want to quit my job, to be _____, is that I know I could get much more money working somewhere else.
6. My father _____ last year and now he spends all his time gardening.
7. We have been _____ for six years, but we've actually known each other for nearly 10 years.
8. My husband's very _____. He buys me flowers every Friday because that's the day we met.
9. Her children are very _____. They never stop bouncing around. I'd love to know where they get their energy from!
10. Who's Petra going out with at the _____?
11. I saw Kim in the market today, by _____.
12. How do you _____ your surname? Is it with one T or two Ts?
13. Sam's really good with figures, so we're both hoping he'll be an _____ when he grows up and look after us in our old age.
14. We've just got a studio _____ at the moment so we're looking for somewhere bigger now that I'm pregnant.
15. My cousin's eldest boy is a _____ footballer down in London.
16. I knew Victoria Beckham before she was _____.

UNIT 5: *Barbara*   59

B Transformations

Change the word in each bracket which Barbara used in her interview to form a word which fills the gap.

1. These aren't wrinkles – they're laughter _____! (line)
2. Stop _____ computer games and go out and get some fresh air! (play)
3. I _____ think you shouldn't wear brown. It doesn't suit your colouring. (honest)
4. I've been working so hard for the last few weeks that last night I stayed in and _____ myself with a hot bath and a tub of ice cream. (indulge)
5. The atmosphere was _____. (electronical)
6. Is Julian going to be at the _____? (met)
7. They say the art of _____ is dead, but I don't believe that for a minute! (romantic)
8. Do you have an _____ with us, madam? (accountant)
9. One of the best things about taking early _____ is that you're still fit enough to do all those things you wanted to do but never had time for when you were working. (retired)
10. Both my sister's children are very _____, but my two are both tone deaf. (musician)
11. I still think teaching is a good _____ for a young woman. (professional)
12. He went to seek his _____ and fortune in Hong Kong when he was a young man. (famous)
13. Have you _____ Petra to the party? (invitations)
14. What's the _____ between Cheddar cheese and Monterey Jack? (different)
15. My cousin works in a hospital in Chicago. He's a _____ in mental health. (specialises)

60   *My Family*

5. Transcript

I: Interviewer **B:** Barbara (3'09")

I: Can I have your full name and address, please?
B: It's Barbara Isenberg.
I: Can you spell 'Isenberg'?
B: I-S-E-N-B-E-R-G.
I: OK. And the first line of your address?
B: It's Linnebornweg . . . 8.
I: Right. And how do you spell 'Linnebornweg'?
B: L-I-double N-E-B-O-R-N-W-E-G.
I: OK. And the postcode?
B: It's double 3, 1, double 0, Paderborn.
I: Right. And how do you spell Paderborn?
B: Paderborn would be P-A-D-E-R-B-O-R-N.
I: OK. And your house telephone number?
B: That's 05251 double 5, double 2, 9.
I: OK. And do you have a mobile phone?
B: No, I haven't got one.
I: Right. Thank you very much.
I: Can you tell me something about your family?
B: Well, I'm married and my husband, he comes from Chile. We've got two children, two boys, aged 14 and 17. They're very **(1) lively** children, very South American, I think. Um, they like to play the computers, not really to work with it. And my husband works in computers as well, so we've got quite a lot of computers in our home.
I: How many have you got?
B: Oh, at the moment I think it's about five.
I: Mmm, hmm. Do you like computers?
B: Well, **(2) to be honest**, not really. I like to work with them, but not to, **(3) to indulge in them**.
I: Mmm. So you don't play games or things like that?
B: No, never. I think I've never, never did that.
I: Do you use them for your work?
B: Yeah, have to.
I: OK. Um, you said your husband's from Chile.
B: He's from Chile, yeah.

I: Why's he . . . why did he come to Germany?
B: He came over on, **(4) on a scholarship** to study electronical engineering over here.
I: Mmm, hmm.
B: Well, and just **(5) by chance** we met and he stayed over here.
I: So you met and **(6) fell in love**.
B: Sort of, yeah. It was a very romantic thing.
I: How long have you been married?
B: It's almost silver wedding. It's twenty, 23? 23 years old.
I: OK. And um, are your mum and dad still alive?
B: They're still alive. And we're quite happy that they are living quite near us in a flat.
I: Mmm, hmm.
B: And my father was an accountant before and now sure he's a **(7) retired** [sic – he's retired].
I: Did your mother ever work?
B: She was a secretary before, but she stopped working when there was the first child.
I: Do you have any brothers and sisters?
B: Yeah. I've got a brother living in Cologne.
I: What does he do?
B: He's working as an organist in church.
I: An organist? He plays the organ? Professional?
B: Professional musician.
I: Mmm, hmm. Is he famous?
B: In his part of the world, yes. (*laughs*) And he loves to write books.
I: Does he travel around much?
B: Mmm, he does.
I: So does he have invitations to play the organ in different towns?
B: Sometimes he has, but at the moment **(8) he specialises in writing books on organs** all over the world, sort of thing.
I: Right.

UNIT 5: *Barbara*

6. Words and Phrases

1. **lively** – full of energy
2. **to be honest** – Here Barbara is telling the interviewer what she really thinks.
3. **to indulge in them** – The verb 'to indulge in something' means to do something you really enjoy, especially something which is considered bad for you. If someone refuses a cream cake or some chocolate because they're on a diet, you could say 'Oh, come on! Indulge yourself!'
4. **on a scholarship** – A sum of money which is given to someone by an educational organisation to help pay for their education. (In Miguel's case he received a scholarship from the University of Paderborn in Germany.)
5. **by chance** – when something happens without being planned
6. **fell in love** – they began to love each other very much
7. **retired** – If someone is retired they have stopped working, usually because of their age. Some people take early retirement and stop working in their 50s or even earlier.
8. **he specialises in writing books on organs** – the specialist subject that he writes books about is organs

A Typical Day

UNIT 6 Andrew

1. Pre-Listening Comprehension

A Schema building

Andrew is 20 and comes from East London. He is a student, but he is currently on a gap year, i.e., he is working for a year in an area related to his degree subject before returning to university. How much do you know about London? Discuss the following statements with a partner and mark them True or False.

1. T   F   London was founded by the Romans in AD43.
2. T   F   The world's first metro system – the London Underground – was created in 1883 and it is still expanding.
3. T   F   The population of London is around 12 million.
4. T   F   Almost a third of the people living in London were born outside the UK.

B Discussion

Discuss the questions in small groups. Share your answers with the class.

1. What else do you know about London?
2. What do you think Andrew does in his free time?
3. Do you know what an East London accent sounds like?

C Normalisation

This exercise is designed to help you get used to Andrew's voice. Listen to the first part of the interview and correct the mistakes in the statements.

1. The interview probably takes place on a weekday morning.
2. It takes Andrew about 20 minutes to get ready to leave for work in the morning.
3. He takes the bus to Finsbury Park station.
4. He usually has to wait five minutes for the train from Finsbury Park.
5. He works in Welwyn Golden City.

A Questions

🎧 92

Andrew talks about a typical workday from start to finish. Listen and answer the questions.

1. We know Andrew leaves home at 7.30 and then takes two trains to get to work, so what mistake does he make about the time he arrives for work?
2. What does he do before he starts work at 9 o'clock?
3. Why hasn't he been having lunch for the last few days?
4. Does he have a cooked meal at lunchtime?
5. How long does he work after lunch?
6. Does he ever do overtime?
7. What time is his train back to Finsbury Park?
8. If he misses that train, what time is the next one?
9. How far is the train station from his workplace?
10. What time does he usually get home from work?
11. Does he cook his own dinner?
12. Who does he sometimes see in the evening?

B Gap-Fill

🎧 93

Andrew talks about what he does in his free time. Before you listen, try to predict which words, or which types of words (nouns, adjectives, pronouns, parts of verbs, etc.), will fit in the gaps. Then listen and check your answers.

1. Because Andrew is on a placement year, he has some _____ to do.
2. The university likes him to keep a _____ which he has to _____ regularly.
3. He has also got to write an _____.
4. If Andrew doesn't go out or study, he'll watch a _____ at home.
5. He has a _____ in his _____ with a games console.
6. He normally goes _____ on a Saturday and sees his _____.
7. Sometimes he goes to the _____ with his friends.
8. If he doesn't go out on a Saturday, that means he must be _____.

66 *A Typical Day*

C Corrections

🎧 94

Andrew talks about the things he gets up to with his friends. Listen to this chunk of text from the interview and correct the 12 pieces of incorrect information:

I: Interview   A: Andrew

I: OK. You said you've got um, you've got three groups of friends. What, what are they – friends from college or friends from university, or . . .?

A: There's . . . well, the friends from university are in Fermingham, but I do go up and see them every now and then, like, like this year, 'cos I'm not in Birmingham this month, obviously. Um, but I've got people from college, got guys that I met er . . . I used to go to scouts and there's people that I still sort of speak to from that and er, other people I've met along the way, that I sort of hang out with.

I: Right. You talked about hanging out in the past. Do you, do you go out dancing or?

A: Oh, um, yeah, we, we'll go to the bar quite a lot er, sort of. By the park I meant like we'll go down the Marshes. Sorry, I should have elaborated on that. We, we'll go down the Marshes and we might play Frisbee or sit around and talk er, to keep ourselves busy really. Just have fun.

I: Not getting into trouble.

A: Not getting into trouble, no! Too good for that.

3. Interesting Language Points

A Colloquial language 1 – *a bit*

🎧 95

We use *a bit* very often in spoken English as a kind of softener, as in this example from the interview:

> Interviewer: *How are you feeling?*
> Andrew: *A bit tired.*

If Andrew just used the word *tired*, that would sound quite abrupt or rude. Look at these other examples:

> Q: *Are you hungry?*   A: *A bit.*

Here the speaker could be thinking: 'Actually I'm starving. I haven't eaten since breakfast.'

> Q: *What's wrong?*   A: *I'm feeling a bit stressed.*

The real meaning could be: 'I've got so much to do at work that I've been working 12 hours a day for the last 10 days. Wouldn't you be stressed?'

> Q: *Do you fancy Paul?*   A: *A bit.*

The real meaning could be: 'Yes, I think he's gorgeous, but I don't want you to know that.'

B Colloquial language 2 – *sort of*

Andrew uses this expression a lot. It is very common in spoken English when we are giving approximate descriptions of things, as in these examples:

> *My bedroom is a sort of blue-grey colour.*
> *She's got sort of medium-brown hair.*
> *The film's a sort of love story and thriller combined.*

We also use *sort of* to describe activities without being too exact:

> 'I was sort of thinking of having a party to celebrate finishing our exams.'
> 'We were having a relaxing sort of evening when suddenly the hospital called.'

Now listen to Andrew's usage of *sort of*:

🎧 96

> *I'm always early every day er, so I have time to sort of . . . that's when I have my breakfast.*
> *Er, and then just sort of relax for a bit...*
> *So I've got a sort of 20-minute gap, sort of, to play with.*

68   *A Typical Day*

> so you get home about half-six, <u>sort of</u> about an hour
>
> they want me to keep a logbook of what I'm doing so I might <u>sort of</u> update that um, and also a separate essay that I have to do so I <u>sort of</u> start work on that a little bit as well
>
> there's people that I still <u>sort of</u> talk to from that and er, other people I've met along the way, that I <u>sort of</u> hang out with
>
> yeah, we'll go to the pub quite a lot er, <u>sort of</u>

C Colloquial language 3 – 'cos

We often say *'cos* in informal spoken English for the simple reason that it's shorter and easier to say than *because*. Listen to these examples from Andrew's interview:

🎧 97

> the past few days I haven't been having lunch <u>'cos</u> it's been very busy
>
> I'm pretty much always out on a Saturday. I'll er, <u>'cos</u> I've got quite a few groups of friends.
>
> I do pop up and see them every now and then, like, like this year, <u>'cos</u> I'm not in Birmingham this year.

D Colloquial language 4 – just

Andrew uses *just* several times in his interview and again this word is very common in informal spoken English. The meaning is often *that's all*, as in these examples from the interview:

🎧 98

> I bring breakfast in from home. Er, and then <u>just</u> sort of relax for a bit ...
>
> If not I'll <u>just</u> sit in and go to bed about 11 and start the whole thing again.
>
> so I sort of start work on that a little bit as well or I <u>just</u> watch a film
>
> We'll go down the Marshes and we might play Frisbee or something. Might sit around and talk. Er, <u>just</u> keep ourselves occupied, really. <u>Just</u> have fun.

Here are some more examples of this usage of *just*:

> 'I don't take sugar in tea, thanks – <u>just</u> milk.'
>
> 'I'll be fine. I'll <u>just</u> sit here and wait for you.'
>
> 'Work was awful today. I <u>just</u> spent all day dealing with customer complaints.'
>
> 'Do you want jam on your toast, or <u>just</u> butter?'
>
> 'We didn't do much this weekend. We <u>just</u> stayed in and relaxed.'

E *takes* with time expressions

When talking about his journey home, Andrew says:

And then it takes about an hour again to get back...

We use *takes* a lot when we are talking about journeys or the time needed to do something. Look at these examples:

'It takes about 20 minutes to get to Oxford Street from here by Tube.'
'How long does it take to get from Edinburgh to Glasgow by train?'

We can also use *take* with pronouns, as in these examples:

'It took them nearly four hours to get home on Friday because of that crash on the M1.'
'It only takes me five minutes to walk to work.'
'It takes him ages to get ready for school in the mornings.'
'It took me half an hour to find my car keys this morning.'
'Whenever we go abroad it takes us a little while to get used to driving on the right.'

F *like/don't like doing* something

Andrew says:

I just don't like staying in.

We often use the *-ing* form of the verb after verbs such as:

like   love   hate   enjoy   adore   prefer

Here are some examples.

'I like living here because there's a lot happening.'
'I love walking around in bare feet in the summer.'
'My father hates driving at night.'
'We enjoy having people to stay.'

G used to do/used to doing something

1. used to do

Andrew says:

> I <u>used to go</u> to scouts . . .

This means it is something he did in the past, probably frequently or for a long time, but not something he does now.

Look at these further examples of *used to*:

> 'When we lived in London we <u>used to go</u> to the theatre at least once a month.'
> 'My grandmother <u>used to make</u> her own bread.'
> 'Paul <u>used to work</u> in that shop over there.'

Now try to come up with your own examples of things you used to do when you were younger.

2. used to doing

We use this expression to talk about present habits, or things we do frequently now, as in these examples:

> 'Shall I drive? I'<u>m used to driving</u> in the dark.'
> 'My husband'<u>s used to coming</u> home and finding me out.'
> 'It took a while, but now I'<u>m used to living</u> on my own.'

H should have done/shouldn't have done something

Andrew says:

> Sorry, I <u>should have elaborated</u> on that.

We use *should have done* and *shouldn't have done* to talk about past actions and what didn't happen, but perhaps should have happened. The meaning in Andrew's example is he feels a bit bad for not explaining more clearly to the interviewer what he meant.

Look at these further examples of *should have* and *shouldn't have done* something:

> 'I <u>should have sent</u> him a birthday card, but I forgot.'
> 'You <u>shouldn't have shouted</u> at him.'
> 'We <u>should have left</u> before the rush hour.'
> 'I <u>should have finished</u> that report a week ago.'
> 'They <u>shouldn't have let</u> you walk home on your own.'

I **The present perfect simple and continuous**

We use the **present perfect simple** to talk about things we have done or have not done during a period of time leading up to the present. Here the focus is on achievement, or lack of it.

We use the **present perfect continuous** to talk about things we have been doing or have not been doing. Here the emphasis is on the activity, or lack of it.

Look at these two examples. The same person could have said either of these sentences, depending on what they wish to emphasise – their personal achievement, or what they've been doing:

'I have written at least 50 emails today.'
'I have been writing emails all day.'

Now look at Andrew's use of these two tenses:

The past few days I <u>haven't been having</u> lunch 'cos <u>it's been</u> very busy.
there's people that I still sort of talk to from that and er, other people <u>I've met</u> along the way . . .

4. Further Listening Practice

A Recognising individual words in a stream of speech – Dictation

🎧 99 to 🎧 103

With a partner, listen and write the sentences or phrases you hear. Check your answers with the class.

1. _____
2. _____
3. _____
4. _____
5. _____

B Features of an East London accent

🎧 104

1. Not pronouncing the initial letter *h-* of words

Andrew often leaves the letter *h-* off at the beginning of words, as in these excerpts:

> That gives me exactly '*alf* an hour to get ready . . .
> I don't usually '*ave* breakfast then
> I take the whole hour if I do '*ave* lunch
> a separate essay that I '*ave* to do

🎧 105

2. The glottal stop

Another feature of the East London accent is the glottal stop. The glottal stop occurs when the speaker constricts his or her throat and blocks the air stream completely. This results in the speaker not pronouncing fully the *-t* sound at the end of words such as *got* or *lot*, or the *-t-* sounds in words such as *bottle* or *kettle*.

Andrew uses a glottal stop instead of the *t* sounds in the following excerpts:

> I *get* up at seven o'clock every day.
> Welwyn Garden *City* where I work
> relax for a *bit*
> the one after that's half an hour *later*
> once I *get* in
> I'm *pretty* much always *out* on a Saturday.

UNIT 6: *Andrew* 73

5. Further Language Development

A Extension exercise   Fill in the blanks in these new sentences with words you heard during Andrew's interview. The words are listed in the box to help you.

> around   bit   bring   busy   gap   get
> hang   just   met   much   pop   ready
> relax   staying   should   update

1. I've __ _____ made a pot of coffee. Would you like a cup?
2. Aren't you _____ to go yet? We said we'd leave 10 minutes ago.
3. How do you _____ to work? Bus or Tube?
4. What would you like me to _____ to the party? I don't want to turn up empty-handed.
5. I find the best way to _____ is to read in the bath.
6. I'm a _____ cold. Can you put the heating on?
7. It's really _____ at work at the moment because so many people are off with 'flu.
8. She's got a two-hour _____ between appointments on Tuesday, so we could have the meeting then.
9. We need to _____ our computer system. We're still using Windows 98.
10. I don't go out now as _____ as I used to when I was a student.
11. I don't like _____ in on a Friday night – do you?
12. I need to _____ out to the shop for some bread, but I'll be back soon.
13. She _____ Pierre when she was on holiday in Paris.
14. Usually on a Saturday night I just _____ out with friends and have a laugh.
15. Sorry, I _____ have told you I'm a vegetarian. I'll be fine with just the salad.
16. We didn't go out in the end. We just sat _____ and talked.

74   *A Typical Day*

B The present perfect simple and the present perfect continuous

Put the verbs in brackets into the present perfect simple or the present perfect continuous, as appropriate.

1. You (wear) _____ that shirt since Monday. I think it needs washing.
2. Jill (lose) _____ 10 kilos since she went on that diet.
3. (see) _____ you _____ the new *Toy Story* film yet?
4. I (try) _____ to write this report since last week and I still (not finish) _____ it.
5. We (not have) _____ a holiday since 2008.
6. Paul (take) _____ a lot of time off work lately. I think I'd better have a word with him.
7. I (have) _____ five interviews this month.
8. We (wait) _____ for hours!
9. Our neighbours (not speak) _____ to us since we complained about their dog barking.
10. I know this will come as a shock, Dad, but I (decide) _____ to quit work and go back to university.
11. Sorry for not getting in touch, but I (feel) _____ a bit low lately.
12. You can go out when you (finish) _____ the washing up.

C Transformations

Change the word in each bracket which Andrew used in his interview to form a word which fits the gap.

1. I don't think your cunning plan is (work) _____!
2. Have you (get) _____ some spare change, please?
3. Oh no! A filling's just fallen out of my (teeth) _____!
4. Is it (usually) _____ to have Yorkshire pudding with roast lamb?
5. Chris is (train) _____ for the New York marathon at the moment.
6. This is the (early) _____ meeting I've ever had.
7. Have you (bring) _____ your swimming trunks?
8. You should try yoga. It's very (relax) _____.
9. These figures need (update) _____ when you've got a moment.
10. My parents (separate) _____ when I was 10.
11. Have you (work) _____ out the answer yet?
12. I haven't (feeling) _____ this tired in ages.

6. Transcript

I: Interviewer **A:** Andrew (3'35")

I: OK, Andrew, you've just come home from work.
A: Yeah!
I: How are you feeling?
A: A bit tired! (*laughs*)
I: A bit tired. OK. Um, it would be very helpful if you could tell me about a typical day.
A: OK. Um, well, I get up at seven o'clock every day.
I: Every day, right.
A: Yeah. That gives me exactly half an hour to get ready, brush, wash my teeth, brush my teeth, sorry! Have a wash, have a shower. Um, I don't usually have breakfast then. Um, I leave at half-seven as I said. Um, get the train to Finsbury Park.
I: Mhm, hmm.
A: Wait there for about 20 minutes, get another train to Welwyn Garden City where I work.
I: Right.
A: Um, once I get into work – that's usually about 20 to 8-ish – I'm always early every day er, so I have time, sort of... that's when I have my breakfast. I bring breakfast in from home. Er, and then just sort of relax for a bit, start work then. Er, at lunch I leave usually about one o'clock um, but the past few days I haven't been having lunch 'cos it's been very busy.
I: Right.
A: Er, and I will usually er, go to either **(1) Greggs** or just a sandwich place, have **(2) a baguette** or something. Er, and I take the whole hour if I do have lunch because, you know, sometimes I don't so I've got to make up for it. Er, get back about two, carry on working till half-five. Er, after that I leave usually exactly on half-five as well and, as I say, sometimes I've had to stay late er, but my train is exactly 10 to six...
I: OK.
A: And the one after that's half an hour later so I like to try and get the 10 to six one. It's only a five-minute walk from work to get there...
I: Oh, right.
A: ...so er, I've got a sort of 20 minute gap, sort of, to play with. And then it takes about an hour again to get back, so you get home about half-six, sort of about an hour. Um, (*laughs*) and once I get in usually my dinner's ready so I'll have dinner then er, and then if I am going to go and see friends I'll go and see friends. If not I'll just sit in and go to bed about 11 and start the whole thing again. (*laughs*)
I: OK. Um, when you, you say you stay at home, what kind of things do you do at home?

A: If I stay at home um, well, 'cos it's... 'cos I'm on **(3) a placement year** I have some **(4) assignments** to do, er, they like to... they want me to keep **(5) a logbook** of what I'm doing so I might sort of update that. (*coughs*) Um, and also a separate **(6) essay** that I have to do so I sort of start work on that a little bit as well or I just watch a film or...
I: OK. Um, have you got a computer in your bedroom?
A: I have a laptop er, games console, as well. But I don't play the games console as much now. Er...
I: Because of all these assignments...
A: All this, yes. I'm out most of the time. Usually I'm out.
I: OK.
A: I'll go out with my friends.
I: Right. So that's a, a typical day working day...
A: Yeah.
I: Yeah. What about um, say at the weekend? What's a typical Saturday like?
A: At the weekend um, **(7) I'm pretty much always out on a Saturday.** I'll er, 'cos I've got quite a few groups of friends.
I: Mmm.
A: And I'm always seeing one of them, so I'll usually be round a friend's house or I'll do something at a friend's house er, it's, yeah, gen... or go down the park, something like this. But I'm always out, pretty much. If I'm not out, I'm ill usually. (*laughs*) Er, I don't like staying in.
I: OK. You said you've got um, you've got different groups of friends. What, what are they – friends from school or friends from university, or...?
A: There's... well, the friends from university are in Birmingham, but **(8) I do pop up and see them every now and then**, like, like this year, 'cos I'm not in Birmingham this year, obviously. Um, but I've got people from college, got people I met er... I used to go to **(9) scouts** and there's people that I still sort of talk to from that and er, other **(10) people I've met along the way, (11) that I sort of hang out with.**
I: Right. You talked about hanging out in the park. Do you, do you go out clubbing or?
A: Oh, um, yeah, we'll go to the pub quite a lot er, sort of. By the park I meant like we'll go down **(12) the Marshes. (13) Sorry, I should have elaborated on that.** We'll go down the Marshes and we might play **(14) Frisbee** or something. Might just sit around and talk. Er, just keep ourselves occupied, really. Just have fun.
I: Not getting into trouble.
A: Not getting into trouble, no! Too old for that.

76   *A Typical Day*

7. Words and Phrases

1. **Greggs** – a famous chain of bakeries found in most city and town centres
2. **baguette** – a large filled roll where the bread is part of a long, thin French loaf
3. a **placement year** – a year when a student takes a year out from their degree course and works in an area related to their degree subject
4. **assignments** – university projects
5. a **logbook** – a record or diary of what he has been doing at work to show his tutors at university
6. (an) **essay** – a long piece of written work which counts as part of his degree coursework
7. **I'm pretty much always out on a Saturday.** – I usually go out on Saturdays.
8. **I do pop up and see them every now and then** – I do go up and see them occasionally, just for a short time. The expression 'to pop in/up/down/into' is very common in spoken English, as in these examples:
   'I just need to pop in next door and feed their cat.'
   'My daughter usually pops over to see me on a Friday.'
   'Could you pop these into the post for me?'
   'Is it OK if I pop round later for a cup of coffee?'
9. **scouts** – an organisation for young boys that teaches them practical skills
10. **people I've met along the way** – people that he's met in different situations during his life so far
11. **that I sort of hang out with** – that I spend my free time with, not doing anything special, just getting together
12. **the Marshes** – A marsh is an area of flat ground near a river or lake. The area where Andrew lives in east London is called Walthamstow and it is famous for the Marshes – a large area rich in wild life situated near the River Lea.
13. **Sorry, I should have elaborated on that.** – Sorry, I should have explained that. (Andrew realises that when he says 'the park' he actually means the Marshes.)
14. **Frisbee** – a circular piece of plastic with a hard edge which is thrown from person to person and which will return to the thrower if thrown in the right way (in the same way a boomerang does)

UNIT 7 Tammy

1. Pre-Listening Comprehension

A Schema building

Tammy is a theatre sister (a senior nurse in charge of an operating theatre) in a busy London hospital. She comes from Canada, but she moved to the UK 17 years ago. How much do you know about Canada? Discuss the following statements with a partner and mark them True or False.

1. T F Canada is the second-largest country in the world in terms of area.
2. T F The population of Canada is around 60 million.
3. T F Nearly 25% of all the fresh water in the world is in Canada.
4. T F The largest city in Canada is Vancouver.
5. T F Forests cover about half of Canada.

B Discussion

Discuss the questions in small groups. Share your answers with the class.

1. What else do you know about Canada?
2. How many hospital-related words do you know?
3. How does the sight of blood (your own or other people's) make you feel?
4. Have you ever had an operation? If so, how did you feel before the operation?
5. What do you think a theatre sister does on a typical workday?
6. Do you know what a Canadian accent sounds like?

C Normalisation

This exercise is designed to help you get used to Tammy's voice. Listen to the first part of the interview and answer the questions.

1. What time does Tammy get up?
2. What pets does she have?
3. What does she do before she gets dressed?
4. Who does she give some milk to, after she's made her coffee?

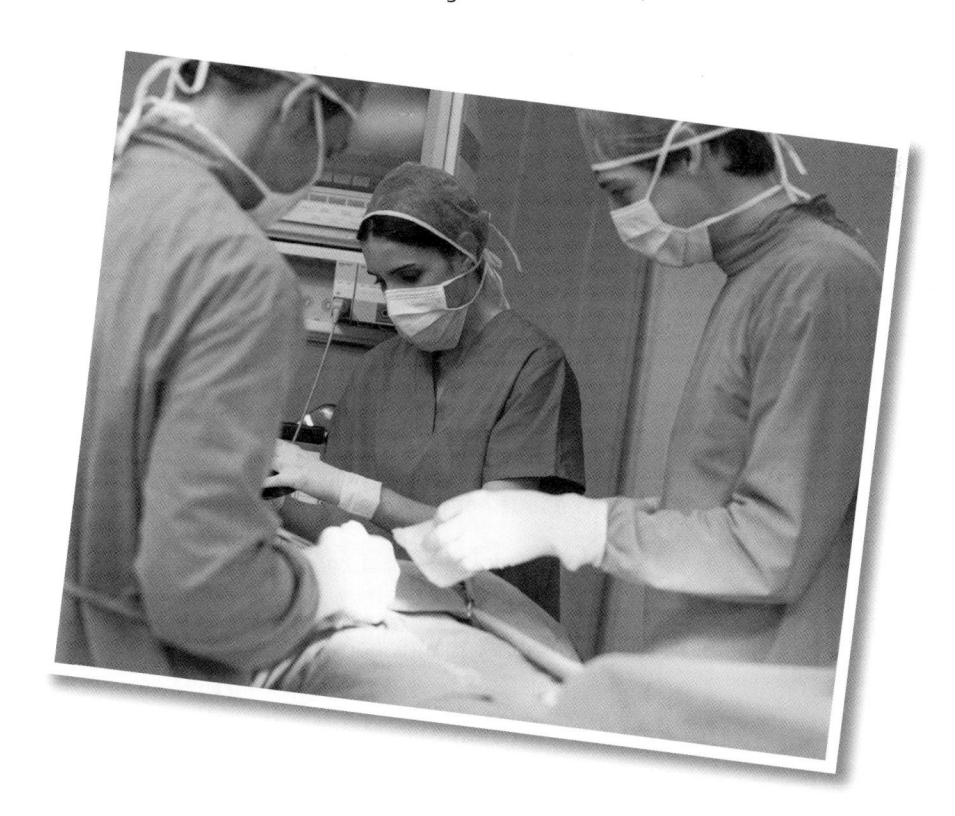

2. Listening Comprehension

A True/False
108

Tammy talks about her mornings. Listen and decide if each statement is True (T) or False (F). Remember to give reasons for your answers.

1. T F Tammy always has breakfast before she goes to work.
2. T F She listens to the radio news every morning.
3. T F She leaves her home at between quarter and ten to eight.
4. T F She knows what operations are planned from the day before.
5. T F She doesn't usually have a break in the morning because she's too busy.

B Gap-Fill
109

Tammy talks about her afternoons. Before you listen, try to predict which words, or which types of words, will fit in the gaps. Then listen and check your answers.

Typically get about 10, 15 minutes for _____

and then get back, back to it and send _____

if I can and try to get _____ through as

quickly and as _____ as possible. Try to have

a bit of a _____ with them 'cos they usually

come up they're quite _____. Er, once the

last patient's _____, I make sure everything's

_____ in Recovery, _____

_____, go _____, take the dogs out

for a _____.

C Questions
110

Tammy talks about her evenings. Listen and answer the questions.

1. What do you think the word *knackered* means in the first full sentence?
2. Which two sports does Tammy play regularly?
3. What is the latest Tammy goes to bed during the week?
4. How much sleep does she get if she's lucky?
5. How much sleep can she usually manage on?

A Typical Day

3. Interesting Language Points

A *it depends on . . .*

When talking about breakfast Tammy says:

Sometimes have breakfast, sometimes don't. It depends on how I feel.

We use *it depends on* when we cannot give a definite answer because the answer could change. In the above example, sometimes Tammy feels like breakfast and sometimes she doesn't. It depends.

Here are some more examples of *it depends on*:

Ann: Shall we have a picnic tomorrow?
Kim: It depends on the weather.

Yura: Can you leave work early tomorrow?
Pat: It depends on how busy we are.

Paul: Do you like tea?
Miko: It depends on what kind of tea it is.

B Combining two verbs

Tammy says:

I sit and watch the morning news.

We often combine two verbs in this way. Here are some more examples:

'Every Thursday I go and play squash at our local sports centre.'
'When I get to the office, I sit and have a coffee at my desk before I start work.'
'On Fridays I usually go out and meet friends.'
'I need to go and do some shopping.'

C *tend to* + verb

Tammy says:

Don't tend to have a break in the morning because it tends to be non-stop.

Here she means she doesn't usually take a break in the mornings because there is always so much to do.

Here are some more examples of *tend to*:

'I tend to eat more in the winter than in the summer.'
'We tend to leave for work at around 8 o'clock most days.'
'My sister tends to go out most Fridays.'
'It tends to rain more in the north of England.'

UNIT 7: *Tammy* **81**

D as . . . as . . .

Tammy says:

I try and get the patients through <u>as quickly and efficiently as</u> possible.

Here are some more examples of *as . . . as . . .*:

'Please eat your breakfast <u>as quickly as</u> you can. You're going to be late for school.'
'We drove here <u>as fast as</u> we could. How are you feeling now?'
'We eat <u>as much fruit as</u> we can, although it does get a bit boring sometimes.'
'I am studying <u>as hard as</u> I can because I really want to get top marks.'

E once/as soon as

Tammy says:

<u>Once</u> the last patient's out I make sure everything's OK in Recovery.

The meaning of *once* in this context is *as soon as*. Look at these examples:

'<u>Once</u> I've passed my driving test I'm going to buy a car.'
'<u>Once</u> we've finished the front room we're going to paint the kitchen.'
'<u>Once</u> I've qualified I'm going to move to the country.'

F depending on

Tammy says:

<u>Depending on</u> how knackered I am, I'll take the dogs for a long walk or a short walk.

The meaning here is that if Tammy's very tired she only takes the dogs for a short walk; but if she's feeling OK, then she takes them for a long walk.

Here are some more examples of *depending on*:

'<u>Depending on</u> the weather, we'll either have a barbecue or we'll eat indoors.'
'<u>Depending on</u> my exam results, I'll either do another course or stop studying all together.'
'<u>Depending on</u> how you feel, we can either go to the cinema or stay in and watch a DVD.'

G Conditional I

Tammy says:

I'll be lucky if I get four hours' sleep.

When we use *if* + **present simple** and *will* + **verb stem**, this is known as a *Conditional I* sentence. There are a lot of different forms of conditional sentences, but here are some more examples of the one above:

'I'll be thrilled if they offer me the job.'
'If the dentist says I need a filling I'll make another appointment.'
'If you eat all that chocolate you'll be sick!'
'I'll be furious if you're late again.'

4. Further Listening Practice

A *'cos* instead of *because* in fast, informal spoken English

(111)

When we are talking quickly, we often say *'cos* instead of *because* as it's shorter and easier to say. Listen to Tammy:

> give the dogs a bit of milk *'cos* that's what they're waiting for
>
> Don't tend to have a break in the morning *'cos* it tends to be non-stop or there's always problems to sort out.

Tammy: *I'll be lucky if I get four hours' sleep.*
Interviewer: *Why?*
Tammy: *'Cos I just don't sleep very well.*

B Two classic intonation patterns

1. Intonation for lists

When we are giving one piece of information after the other, the standard intonation pattern is for the voice to rise with each piece of information and to fall on the final piece of information. This final fall occurs to alert the listener to the fact that the list of information has come to an end. Listen to your teacher reading out the following example:

> *'I need six first-class stamps, two second-class stamps, one stamp for a letter to Europe and one 69p stamp.'*

Now look at these examples and predict with arrows (↗ ↘) where you will hear a rise or fall. Then listen to your teacher reading the examples aloud and check your answers.

> 'We'd like three coffees, two teas, and a Coke, please.'
>
> 'I know Germany quite well. I've been to Berlin, Hamburg, Dresden, and Leipzig.'

2. Intonation for statements

The standard intonation pattern with statements is for the voice to fall at the end, although many younger British native speakers, New Zealanders, Canadians, and Americans often go up at the end of statements.

When Tammy is giving various pieces of information about a typical day, her voice tends to rise each time. However, towards the end of the interview her voice falls when she is making statements. The following exercise is designed to train you to identify whether you hear a rise or fall in the speaker's intonation:

Listen and mark with arrows (↗ ↘) whether you hear a rise or fall at the end of each statement:

84 *A Typical Day*

112

1. get up about quarter to seven
2. might go to rugby, depending on how I'm feeling
3. I get up and have a shower and then I get dressed
4. and then go to bed
5. give the dogs a bit of milk 'cos that's what they're waiting for
6. sit and watch the morning news
7. I'll be lucky if I get four hours' sleep
8. once I get to work I find out what we're doing

C Features of a Canadian accent 1: *en* instead of *and*

Canadians and Americans tend to say *en* rather than *and* in fast informal speech. Listen again to Tammy:

113

I get up <u>and</u> have a shower
then get back, back to it <u>and</u> send early if I can <u>and</u> try to get patients through as quickly <u>and</u> as efficiently as possible

D Features of a Canadian accent 2: leaving off the final *-g* of words ending in *-ing*

Some Canadians and Americans tend not to pronounce the find *-g* in rapid speech. Listen to Tammy:

114

OK. I get up about quarter to seven in the <u>mornin'</u>. The dogs don't wake me up. They don't get out of bed till I make coffee.
I sit and watch the <u>mornin'</u> news...

E Features of a Canadian accent 3: *'em* instead of *them* in fast speech

Instead of saying *them* in rapid speech, Canadians, Americans, and many British speakers often shorten this to *'em*. Listen again to Tammy:

115

Depending on how knackered I am, I'll take <u>'em</u> for a long walk or a short walk.

F Features of a Canadian accent 4: *couple of* and *coffee*

Instead of saying *couple of* in rapid speech, Canadians, Americans and many British speakers shorten this to *coupla*. Listen again to Tammy:

116

It's just I only need a <u>coupla</u> [couple of] hours usually...

Canadians and Americans tend to put a lot more stress on the first syllable of *coffee* than British English speakers. Listen again to Tammy:

117

they don't get out of bed till I make <u>coffee</u>

UNIT 7: *Tammy* 85

G **Recognising individual words in a stream of speech – Dictation**

🎧 118 to 🎧 124

With a partner, listen and write the sentences or phrases you hear. Check your answers with the class.

1. _____
2. _____
3. _____
4. _____
5. _____
6. _____
7. _____

H **Recognising sentence stress**

🎧 125

Stressed words are the most important in spoken English because they carry the most meaning. Which words do you think Tammy stresses in the following extracts?

1. *I get up about quarter to seven in the morning.*
2. *I get up and have a shower.*
3. *give the dogs a bit of milk*
4. *there's always problems to sort out*
5. *typically get about 10, 15 minutes for lunch*
6. *try to have a bit of a laugh with them*
7. *I'll be lucky if I get four hours' sleep.*

Now listen to find out if your predictions were correct.

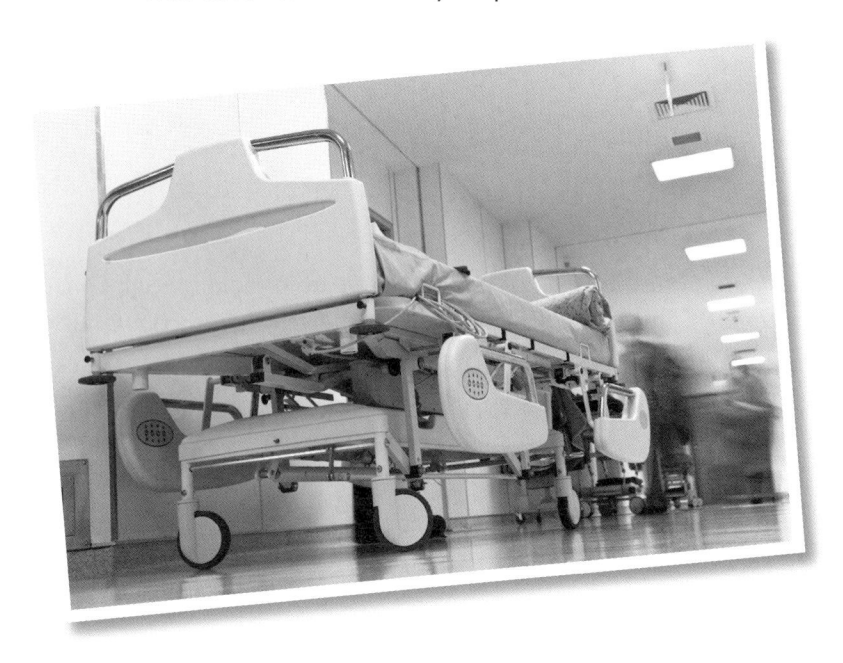

5. Further Language Development

A Extension exercise Fill in the blanks in these new sentences with words you heard during Tammy's interview. The words are listed in the box to help you. One of the words is used twice.

> as   catches   changed   depending   depends
> dressed   finish   get   going   knackered   laugh
> once   out   problems   scared   tend   wake   walk

1. I want to hear all about your holiday from start to _____.
2. Please don't _____ me up before 10 o'clock.
3. I only _____ out of bed when my husband's finished in the shower.
4. On a Sunday I don't get _____ after my shower. I just put on my dressing gown.
5. I don't go out every Friday – it _____ on what kind of day I've had.
6. Why are the police here? What's _____ on?
7. I _____ to get home at about 6 o'clock most days.
8. Simone has a few problems she needs to sort _____. She'll be joining us later.
9. How long do you _____ for lunch at your place?
10. Please be as quiet _____ you can. I don't want the kids to wake up.
11. I know Rob seems a bit scary at first, but you can really have a _____ with him when you get to know him. He's really funny.
12. My sister is so _____ of going to the dentist that she tends to put off going for ages, even if she's in pain.
13. _____ I've finished doing the ironing I'm going out in the garden.
14. Why do I need to get _____? It's only a barbecue.
15. _____ on how I feel when I get up, I either walk or drive to work.
16. I'm not coming out tonight – I'm too _____.
17. We went for a _____ in the forest on Sunday. It was too hot to run.
18. I've been having _____ reading small print. I think I need to get glasses.
19. I can manage a couple of nights without much sleep, but then it _____ up with me.

UNIT 7: Tammy   87

B Transformations

Change the word in each bracket which Tammy used in her interview to form a word which fits the gap.

1. Have the kids (wake) _____ up yet?
2. The weather forecast said we'd have sunny spells and (shower) _____ today.
3. I used to love (dress) _____ up in my mother's clothes when I was a girl.
4. Do you want to have my coffee instead? It's too (milk) _____ for me.
5. Have you (find) _____ out where it is yet?
6. I spent the weekend (sort) _____ out my clothes for the holiday.
7. Can you walk a bit (quickly) _____? I said we'd be there by 8.
8. Stop (laugh) _____ at me!
9. What's the (scared) _____ film you've ever seen?
10. Where's the (change) _____ room, please?
11. I left my keys at work yesterday, but (lucky) _____ Sam was in when I got home.
12. I had a great holiday, but Dominic (catches) _____ a cold, so he was a bit miserable.
13. Have you got any aspirin? I think I am (get) _____ a headache.

C The first conditional

Put the verbs in brackets into the simple present or future simple, as appropriate, using contractions wherever possible.

1. If I (see) _____ another dress like it I (get) _____ it for your birthday.
2. I (bring) _____ the salad if you (get) _____ the meat.
3. If you (want) _____ to go home I (give) _____ you a lift.
4. I'm sure it (be) _____ cheaper if we (go) _____ by car.
5. If you (get) _____ to the station before 9.30, they (not let) _____ you use your travelcard.
6. I (bring) _____ your book back next week if I (remember) _____.
7. If I (see) _____ Siri I (tell) _____ her you were asking after her.
8. I (give) _____ you $100 if you (pass) _____ your driving test.
9. If the tickets (cost) _____ more than £20 I (not go) _____.
10. If you (stay) _____ in the sun too long you (get) _____ sunstroke.

D Phrasal verbs

Insert the following phrasal verbs taken from Tammy's interview into the gaps:

> catch up   find out   get up
> wait for   sort out   wake up

1. I need to _____ early tomorrow because I've got a doctor's appointment at 8.15.
2. _____! You're snoring!
3. Can you _____ me? I've just got to make a quick phone call.
4. I need to stay in tonight because I've got to _____ on some work.
5. Did you _____ what time the train leaves?
6. I really need to _____ this drawer. I can't find anything.

6. Transcript

I: Interviewer **T:** Tammy (1'54")

T: Typical day.
I: From start to finish.
T: OK. I get up about quarter to seven in the morning. The dogs don't wake me up. They don't get out of bed till I make coffee. I get up and have a shower and then I get dressed, make coffee er, give the dogs a bit of milk 'cos that's what they're waiting for. Er, sometimes have breakfast, sometimes don't, depends on how I feel. I sit and watch the morning news, find out what's going on, and then er, I go to work about quarter to eight, ten to eight. Er, once I get to work I find out what we're doing, who I'm going to have in theatre with me. Er, **(1) try to sort out all the problems, (2) get all the kit up,** send for the first **(3) patient** as soon as it's ready, and go from there. **(4) Don't tend to have a break in the morning** 'cos **(5) it tends to be non-stop** or **(6) there's always problems to sort out.** Typically get about 10, 15 minutes for lunch and then get back, back to it and **(7) send early if I can** and try to get patients through as quickly and as efficiently as possible. **(8) Try to have a bit of a laugh with them** 'cos [when] they usually come up they're quite scared. Er, once the last patient's out, I make sure everything's OK in **(9) Recovery, (10) get changed**, go home, take the dogs out for a walk. Depending on how **(11) knackered** I am, I'll take 'em out for a long walk or a short walk. Um, depending on what day it is I'll go do . . . either **(12) go for a run**, go and play hockey, might go to rugby depending on how I'm feeling. Er, and then go to bed.
I: What time do you normally go to bed?
T: About 11.30, 12, depending.
I: So do you always try and have eight hours' sleep?
T: I'll be lucky if I get four hours' sleep!
I: Why?
T: 'Cos I just don't sleep very well.
I: Have you always had problems sleeping?
T: Um, yeah, yeah, definitely. It's not . . . It's . . . It's just I only need a couple hours usually so . . . **(13) It catches up to me** and then I have a, one night where I'll have six to eight hours and then I'll er, be OK again for a while.

90 *A Typical Day*

7. Words and Phrases

1. **try to sort out all the problems** – I try to deal with all the problems; I try to solve all the problems
2. **get all the kit up** – kit is an informal word for equipment. Here Tammy is talking about the equipment needed for the operations. The equipment comes from a special department in the basement, one floor below the operating theatres, which is why Tammy says *up*.
3. **patient** – a person who is receiving treatment in hospital
4. **Don't tend to have a break in the morning** – I don't usually have a break
5. **it tends to be non-stop** – it (i.e. the work) usually goes on and on without a pause
6. **There's always problems to sort out** – there are always problems to deal with
7. **send early if I can** – Tammy means she sends a porter to bring the next patient from the ward to the operating theatre as soon as possible
8. **Try to have a bit of a laugh with them** – I try to laugh and joke with them (i.e. she tries to put the patients at their ease and make them feel less stressed.)
9. **Recovery** – After their operations, the patients are taken to a special room where they are monitored until they regain consciousness.
10. **get changed** – I change my clothes. Tammy takes off her theatre greens and puts on her ordinary clothes before she goes home.
11. **knackered** – an informal word meaning very tired (NB not very polite!)
12. **go for a run** – go jogging
13. **It catches up to me** – Here the meaning is that Tammy can exist on very little sleep for days at a time, but eventually *it catches up to me* and she needs to have a really good night's sleep. (NB In British English we normally say *it catches up with me*.)

UNIT 7: *Tammy*

UNIT 8 Caroline and Martin

1. Pre-Listening Comprehension

A Discussion

Caroline and Martin both do backstage theatre work in London, working behind the scenes on lighting, sound, and so on. Caroline is 23 and speaks with an RP accent. Martin is 27 and speaks with a South Welsh accent. They met while they were studying to become theatre technicians at RADA (the Royal Academy of Dramatic Art in London). Discuss the questions in small groups. Share your answers with the class.

1. How many theatre-related words can you think of?
2. What hours do you expect Caroline and Martin to work?
3. What are the advantages and disadvantages of working in the theatre?
4. Caroline and Martin recently moved back to London from Leicester in the Midlands – the centre of England. What are their possible reasons for moving?

A Typical Day

B Normalisation

This exercise is designed to help you get used to Caroline and Martin's voices. Listen to the first part of the interview and answer the questions.

1. What time did Caroline and Martin start work at the theatre in Leicester?
2. What time did Martin normally wake up when he was living in Leicester?
3. How many days a week did Caroline and Martin work in Leicester?
4. What was the maximum number of hours they worked per week in Leicester?

UNIT 8: *Caroline and Martin*

2. Listening Comprehension

A True/False

Caroline and Martin talk about their work in London. Answer True or False. Be prepared to give reasons for your answers.

1. T F Caroline and Martin live in a flat.
2. T F Martin is working on a show called "Priscilla" in London's East End.
3. T F Caroline sometimes works in the same theatre as Martin.
4. T F Martin works even longer hours in London than he did in Leicester.
5. T F Occasionally Martin has to start work at 10am.
6. T F Caroline only has one day off a week.
7. T F Sometimes Caroline just works two hours in the morning at the Royal Opera House.
8. T F Caroline has problems sleeping.
9. T F Caroline usually drives into work.
10. T F Sometimes Martin doesn't get up until 1pm.
11. T F Caroline and Martin always have breakfast together.

B Gap-Fill

Caroline and Martin talk about meeting up for lunch. Before you listen, try to predict which words, or which **types** of words, will fit in the gaps. Then listen and check your answers.

1. If Caroline's working at the Royal Opera House she has an hour's _____ from _____ pm and sometimes Martin's _____ at the same time.
2. They often meet on a _____ because Martin finishes his maintenance work by _____ pm and Caroline is free between 6 and _____ pm.
3. They have dinner in the Royal Opera House canteen because they get served quickly, it's nice and _____ and there is a great _____.
4. From the Royal Opera House canteen you can see the London _____ and Big _____.
5. It normally takes Martin about _____ minutes to walk to the Royal Opera House from his theatre.
6. On a Saturday it takes him longer because the streets are so _____.
7. After they finish work, they travel home by _____.

94 *A Typical Day*

8. They get to back to Walthamstow at about _____pm.
9. Every night when they get home they watch a programme called _____ _____.
10. The last thing they do before they go to _____ is _____ their_____.
11. Martin has to work at weekends, but Caroline normally has _____ off.
12. Sometimes Caroline has to work _____.

C Note-taking

Caroline talks about what she did last Saturday and Sunday.
Take notes and then compare your version with other people in the class.

_____
_____
_____
_____
_____
_____
_____

UNIT 8: *Caroline and Martin* 95

3. Interesting Language Points

A *would do something* for past habit

We use *would* + verb when we are talking about things we did regularly in the past. The meaning is the same as *used to do something*. Look at these examples:

'When I was at school, I would stay late every Thursday to play tennis.'
'When Max was a puppy, he would bark all night.'

Remember that *would* is often shortened to *'d*, as in:

'I'd never get up when I was a kid until mum had shouted at least twice.'

Now look at these examples from the interview, when Martin is talking about his previous job in Leicester:

Interviewer: *So what time would you get up in the morning, then?*
Martin: *I'd be in for 9 o'clock on a normal day, so I'd wake up at about half-seven.*
Martin: *And then the normal day'd go through then till 10 o'clock at night.*

B *will do something* and *won't do something* for current habits

We use *will* + verb stem and *won't* + verb stem to talk about things that happen regularly in the present. Look at these examples. Remember *will* is often shortened to *'ll* and *will not* is often shortened to *won't*.

'On a Sunday we'll usually go out for dinner.'
'The children will play in the garden all day in the summer.'
'We'll usually go to France about three times a year.'

Now look at these examples from the interview when Martin is talking about his current job:

The working day normally won't start until about 2 o'clock.
Sometimes I won't be in till half-six in the evening.
generally without fail we'll finish at about half-ten at night

C *have to do something/ had to do something* (external obligation)

We use *have to* or *had to do something* when we feel we are obliged or forced to do something that we don't really want to do. Look at these examples:

> 'I have to get up early tomorrow because I've got to pick up a customer from the airport.'
> 'We have to pay £90 a year just to park our car outside our house in London.'
> 'My dad had to do the cooking and cleaning when we were young because mum had to work such long hours.'

Now look at these examples of *have to do something* and *had to do something* from the interview:

> Some days I have to go in for 10 o'clock in the morning.
> And you have to get the Tube to work?
> We have to finish at about . . . 2.30.
> I don't have to be back for the show till about 7 o'clock . . .
> And then we had to take the set down.

D *'cos* and *till* instead of *because* and *until* in informal spoken and written English

131 to 132

When we are speaking or writing informally, we often shorten *because* to *'cos* and *until* to *till*. Look at these examples from the interview:

1. *'cos*

   Interviewer: Is that 'cos you can't sleep, or . . .
   Caroline: We go to the Opera House canteen 'cos it's . . . we get served there quickly 'cos it's obviously . . .
   Martin: Yes.
   Caroline: . . . in-house.

2. *till*

   Martin: And then the normal day'd go through then till 10 o'clock at night.
   Martin: Sometimes I won't be in till half-six in the evening . . .
   Caroline: a lot of it's 9 o'clock in the morning till 10 o'clock at night

UNIT 8: *Caroline and Martin*

E Signalling that the person listening is paying attention

We use words such as *OK* and *Right* to signal that we're paying attention to a speaker, as well as the sounds *Mmm* and *Mmm, hmm*. Look at these examples from the interview:

1. *Right*

   Martin: *I'd be in for 9 o'clock on a normal day, so I'd wake up at about half-seven?*
   Interviewer: *Right.*

   Martin: *Er, we were on a set contract so they could . . . er, we could work up to 49 hours every week . . .*
   Interviewer: *Right.*
   Martin: *. . . for a set salary.*

   Interviewer: *So you're going in earlier than Martin is, generally.*
   Caroline: *Yeah.*
   Interviewer: *Right.*
   Martin: *Yeah.*

2. *OK*

   Martin: *Um, some days I have to go in for 10 o'clock in the morning, but it's very rare.*
   Interviewer: *OK.*

   Caroline: *We go home together.*
   Interviewer: *On the Tube?*
   Caroline: *Yeah.*
   Martin: *Yes.*
   Interviewer: *OK.*

   Caroline: *So we go home, watch that. Sometimes have a pint at the pub.*
   Interviewer: *OK.*

3. *Mmm* and *Mmm, hmm*

   Martin: *The working day normally won't start until about 2 o'clock.*
   Interviewer: *Mmm.*

   Caroline: *It depends on, on what I'm supposed to be doing.*
   Interviewer: *Mmm.*

   Caroline: *There's a lot of days at the moment where I'm starting work at 9 or 10 in the morning.*
   Interviewer: *Mmm.*

98 *A Typical Day*

Martin:		*Leave at about half-past eight to be in and ready to start work at 9.*
Interviewer:		*Mmm, hmm.*

Caroline:		*I get up er, oh, well, I tend to get up about 8 . . .*
Interviewer:		*Mmm, hmm.*
Caroline:		*. . . 7 o'clock in the morning.*

F Expressing surprise when listening

🎧 136

We often use the word *Really?* with falling intonation to express surprise. Listen to these examples:

1. ***Really?***

Caroline:		*Or ridiculously long days, from 9 in the morning till 10 at night.*
Interviewer:		*Really?*

Martin:		*And then the normal day'd go through then till 10 o'clock at night.*
Interviewer:		*Wow!*
Caroline:		*Six days a week.*
Martin:		*Six days a week.*
Interviewer:		*Really?*

Another way of expressing surprise is using the word *Wow!* or *Gosh!* Listen to these examples:

🎧 137

2. ***Wow!* and *Gosh!***

Martin:		*And then the normal day'd go through then till 10 o'clock at night.*
Interviewer:		*Wow!*

Martin:		*I work with the scenery backstage um, on a show called "Priscilla" in the West End of London.*
Interviewer:		*Oh, wow!*

Interviewer:		*So you worked 20 hours, or more.*
Caroline:		*Yeah.*
Interviewer:		*Gosh!*

UNIT 8: *Caroline and Martin* **99**

G The fillers *er* and *um*

🎧 138

We use the fillers *er* and *um* as a way of giving ourselves time to think while we are in a speaking situation. These fillers signal to the other listener(s) that 'I am thinking, so don't interrupt!' Listen to these examples.

- *er* and *um*

    Interviewer: *So what time would you get up in the morning, then?*
    Martin: *Um, on a normal day ...*

    Interviewer: *Did you get overtime for that?*
    Martin: *No.*
    Caroline: *No. (laughs)*
    Martin: *No. Er, we were on a set contract so they could ... er, we could work up to 49 hours every week ...*

    Interviewer: *Now what are you working as now?*
    Martin: *Er, I work with the scenery backstage um, on a show called Priscilla in the West End of London.*

    Interviewer: *What time do you start?*
    Caroline: *Um, well last Saturday it was fun. I started at 10 o'clock in the morning – Saturday morning. Um, and then I worked through till half-past two.*
    Interviewer: *Right.*
    Caroline: *Um, then I had a three-hour break um, and then I went down into the studio theatre at the Opera House ...*

100 *A Typical Day*

4. Further Listening Practice

A Features of spoken English: elision and the glottal stop stress

(139)

When speaking quickly in English, people often miss out individual sounds at the ends of words – a process known as *elision*. For example, a speaker will say *las' night* instead of *last night*, *jus' got here* instead of *just got here*, or *trie' to* instead of *tried to*.

Another feature of natural spoken English is the glottal stop. The glottal stop occurs when the speaker constricts his or her throat and blocks the air stream completely. This results in the speaker not pronouncing fully the *-t* sound at the end of words such as *got* or *lot*, or the *-t-* sounds in words such as *bottle* or *kettle*.

This gap-fill exercise focuses on words which you probably know already, but whose pronunciation has changed because of *elision* or Caroline and Martin's use of the *glottal stop*.

Listen to these excerpts and insert the missing words.

1. you've recently _____ _____ to London, I think
2. Sometimes I _____ _____ in till half-six in the evening.
3. It depends on, on _____ I'm _____ _____ be doing.
4. I _____ _____ er, oh, well, I _____ _____ get up _____ 8 . . .
5. There's a _____ of days at the moment where I'm starting work at 9 or 10 in the morning.
6. Sometimes, if I've _____ _____ the _____ _____, um, and I _____ _____ to be in till much later, then I'll leave it until _____ midday or one o'clock.
7. the cut-off time is _____ 2.30, so I _____ an hour's _____ _____
8. so we've _____ _____ an hour to _____ with each other
9. We _____ _____ _____ quickly.
10. And then I _____ _____ till half-past two
11. and then I _____ _____ into the studio theatre _____ the Opera House
12. and then we _____ _____ take the _____ _____ and _____ _____ in a um, in a lorry

UNIT 8: *Caroline and Martin*

13. and we _____ _____ _____ of there... didn't _____ home until 7 o'clock in the morning

14. So I _____ _____ because you're buzzing _____ the end of a night _____ _____.

B Contractions

(140)

Contractions are common in informal spoken and written English, such as two friends chatting, emails between friends, and so on, but not in more formal English such as lectures, speeches, and letters to companies. What is the contracted form of the following words? How do you pronounce the contracted forms?

> do not   did not   I have   we have
> you have   it is   that is   I am   was not   I will
> we will   will not   I would

Look at the following excerpts from the interview and put in the appropriate contractions. Then listen and check your answers.

1. Now um, you two, _____ recently moved back to London, I think, from Leicester . . .

2. We _____ live too far away so it _____ too bad, was it?

3. No, _____ be in for 9 o'clock on a normal day, so _____ wake up at about half-seven?

4. The working day normally _____ start until about 2 o'clock.

5. but generally without fail _____ finish at about half-ten at night

6. a lot of _____ 9 o'clock in the morning till 10 o'clock at night

7. If _____ at the Opera House sometimes I start at 7.30 in the morning . . .

8. it just depends on what job _____ doing

9. Sometimes, if _____ worked later the night before, um, and I _____ need to be in till much later, then _____ leave it until about midday or one o'clock.

10. So you _____ have breakfast together.

11. so _____ got about an hour to spend with each other

12. Oh, _____ your favourite programme?

13. _____ normally free on a Sunday. _____ normally my day off.

14. I _____ awake for all 20 hours.

102   *A Typical Day*

C Recognising individual words in a stream of speech 1 – Dictation

🎧 141 to 🎧 149

Work with a partner. Listen to the excerpts from Caroline and Martin's interview and write them down. Then check with another pair.

1. _____
2. _____
3. _____
4. _____
5. _____
6. _____
7. _____
8. _____
9. _____

D Recognising individual words in a stream of speech 2 – Simplification

🎧 150 to 🎧 154

When we speak quickly a process known as *simplification* occurs. The speaker cuts corners and doesn't articulate words clearly. This makes it difficult to recognise even words that you know.

Listen to your teacher read out the following words from the interview:

opera   generally   especially   supposed   obviously

Now listen to these excerpts. How has the pronunciation of these words changed in a stream of speech?

1. *I also work at the Royal **Opera** House in Covent Garden...*
2. *but **generally** without fail we'll finish at about half-ten at night...*
3. *that's a hassle, **especially** at that time in the morning*
4. *It depends on, on what I'm **supposed** to be doing.*
5. *...but not... **obviously** not on a Thursday*

UNIT 8: *Caroline and Martin* 103

E Recognising individual words in a stream of speech 3 – Weak Forms

Some of the most frequently occurring words in English are the functional (or grammatical) words and many of these have so-called *weak forms*. These weak forms are short, unstressed, and contain weak vowels. Often the vowels are replaced by the schwa /ə/.

The frequent use of weak forms in spoken English makes it difficult for you to recognise words which often have a very important grammatical function. The purpose of this exercise is a) to help you recognise weak forms in spoken English and b) to encourage you to use weak forms yourselves so that your spoken English sounds more fluent.

1. *for*
Listen to your teacher's pronunciation of the word *for* in isolation. Now listen to these excerpts which include the word *for*. What has happened to the word?

2. *and*
Listen to your teacher's pronunciation of the word *and* in isolation. Now listen to these excerpts which include the word *and*. What has happened to the word?

3. *to*
Listen to your teacher's pronunciation of the word *to* in isolation. Now listen to these excerpts which include the word *to*. What has happened to the word?

4. *from*
Listen to your teacher's pronunciation of the word *from* in isolation. Now listen to these excerpts which include the word *from*. What has happened to the word?

Next write out four informal sentences featuring these four weak forms – as might occur in a conversation – and read out your sentences. Make sure you pronounce the weak form naturally.

5. Further Language Development

A Extension exercise

Fill in the blanks in these new sentences with words you heard during Caroline and Martin's interview. The words are listed in the box to help you. Two of the words are used twice.

> add   break   contract   get up   hassle   have
> lazy   overtime   ready   recently   rush   salary
> sharing   supposed   tend   too bad

1. I've been putting on a lot of weight _____ so I need to go on a diet.
2. We _____ to _____ early tomorrow morning to catch our flight to Moscow.
3. It's _____ you can't make it to the party.
4. Are you _____ to leave yet?
5. If we do _____ on a Saturday we get paid double.
6. According to my _____ I should work a maximum of 35 hours a week, but my boss seems to have forgotten that.
7. Because I'm not used to getting a _____ every month, I generally run out of money by the third week.
8. We're driving down together and _____ the cost of the petrol.
9. Aren't you _____ to be at work today?
10. We _____ to spend Christmas with my parents and New Year's with Andre's parents.
11. It's a bit of a _____ getting to my dentist because he lives on the other side of London so you _____ to take the Tube and then two buses to get there.
12. What do you get if you _____ £11.50 to £16.25?
13. I'm _____ to finish work at 5, but I often work later to avoid travelling home during the _____ hour.
14. Our cat is so _____! He just sleeps all day, apart from when he's eating.
15. Why don't you have a _____? You've been working on that report for hours.

UNIT 8: *Caroline and Martin*

B Transformations

Change the word in each bracket which Caroline and Martin used in their interview to form a word which fits the gap.

1. Would you mind (move) _____ your feet so I can sit down?
2. The surgeon who (performances) _____ the operation used to work with my father.
3. I think it's (ridiculously) _____ that the Tubes in London stop running so early at night.
4. (Live) _____ would be very boring without the Internet.
5. We are (contract) _____ to work a 35-hour week.
6. We weren't very hungry so we just (share) _____ a pizza.
7. What (varies) _____ is your dog?
8. I very (rare) _____ go out during the week because I'm always too tired.
9. We're not sure if we can get tickets for that day. We need to check the (available) _____.
10. The (served) _____ was appalling! We had to wait nearly an hour for our starters.
11. Sam seems much more (relaxing) _____ now that he's changed jobs, don't you think?
12. I prefer watching football on telly rather than going to matches because I don't like (crowded) _____.
13. As I was (steps) _____ off the sidewalk my shoe came off and then a car ran over it!
14. We normally do our (feed) _____ shopping in the local supermarket.
15. It was supposed to be a comedy, but I didn't find it very (fun) _____.

C Prepositions and adverbs

Insert the correct preposition or adverb from the list below into the gaps. Some are used several times.

> about   as   at   back   between   by   for   from
> of   off   on   out   over   through   to   until   with

1. We're thinking _____ going to Spain _____ our next holiday.
2. Why don't you give me a call _____ the morning when you know what's happening?
3. I normally go shopping _____ a Thursday.
4. Yesterday I worked _____ 10pm.
5. I start work at 8 and then I work _____ to lunchtime without a break.
6. I'm only _____ a temporary contract _____ the moment so I've started to apply _____ other jobs.
7. What does your boyfriend work _____?
8. I'm working _____ a new project at work which is very exciting.
9. We're having dinner _____ friends tomorrow, but we're free _____ Saturday.
10. I normally get _____ work _____ 9 _____ the latest.
11. Would you like to go _____ _____ me?
12. Why don't you come _____ to our place tonight?
13. Make sure you get back _____ time _____ dinner!
14. Our friends have got a cottage _____ the middle of the village _____ Romsey, so we often go and visit them.
15. The hotel was wonderful. We could see the sea _____ our window!
16. Anneke's just got _____ from Chile. I can't wait to hear all _____ her trip.
17. I normally have one day _____ a month.
18. Don't be sad! It's not the end _____ the world!
19. Can you put your suitcase _____ the car? It's nearly time to go.
20. I was sitting _____ Jack and Bernie so there wasn't a lot _____ room.

UNIT 8: *Caroline and Martin*

6. Transcript

I: Interviewer **C:** Caroline **M:** Martin (6'50")

I: Now um, you two, you've recently moved back to London, I think, from **(1) Leicester** – you were both working up there.
C: Yes.
M: Yeah.
I: So... so theatre – so evening **(2) performances**, **(3) I guess**.
C: Yeah.
I: And...
C: Or **(4) ridiculously long days**, from 9 in the morning till 10 at night. (laughs)
I: Really?
C: Yeah.
M: Yes.
I: For both of you?
C: Yes.
M: Yeah.
I: OK. So what time would you get up in the morning then?
M: Um, on a normal day...
C: We didn't live too far away so it wasn't too bad, was it?
M: No, I'd be in for 9 o'clock on a normal day, so I'd wake up at about half-seven?
I: Right.
M: 8 o'clock sometimes if it was a late one.
C: Mostly 8 o'clock. (laughs)
M: Um...
C: Leave at half-past eight.
M: Leave at about half-past eight to be in and ready to start work at 9.
I: Mmm, hmm.
M: And then the normal day'd go through then till 10 o'clock at night.
I: Wow!
C: Six days a week.
M: Six days a week.
I: Really?
M: Yeah.
I: **(5) Did you get overtime for that?**
M: No.
C: No. (laughs)
M: No. Er, we were on **(6) a set contract** so they could... er, we could work up to 49 hours every week...
I: Right.
M: ...for **(7) a set salary**.
I: Uh, huh. OK. And then you've both moved back to London...
C: Yeah.
I: ...and you're sharing a house together.
M: Yeah.
C: Yeah.

I: Now what are you working as now?
M: Er, I work with **(8) the scenery backstage** um, on a show called "Priscilla" in the West End of London.
I: Oh, wow! OK.
C: And I do... I work there as well doing the lighting and I also work at **(9) the Royal Opera House in Covent Garden** doing the lighting on the main stage and in their **(10) studio theatre** as well.
I: OK. Um, Martin, is it still the same long hours? Do you start at 9 and finish at 10, or...?
M: No, much shorter. Um, now generally I won't... The working day normally won't start until about 2 o'clock.
I: Mmm.
M: Um, some... **(11) It varies through the week.** Sometimes I won't be in till half-six in the evening...
I: Mmm, hmm.
M: ...or afternoon. Um, some days I have to go in for 10 o'clock in the morning, but it's very rare.
I: OK.
M: Um, but generally **(12) without fail** we'll finish at about half-ten at night, so **(13) the hours have shifted much more towards** eve... the evenings.
I: OK. And is that the same for you, Caroline?
C: Er... no! (laughs) I still do a six-day week um... Mostly... a lot of it's 9 o'clock in the morning till 10 o'clock at night. **(14) It depends on, on what I'm supposed to be doing.**
I: Mmm.
C: Like if I'm at the Opera House sometimes I start at 7.30 in the morning and finish at 10.30 at night. If I'm on 'Priscilla" then I start at 6.30 in the evening and finish at 10 o'clock at night, so that's... it just depends on what job I'm doing.
I: So what time do you get up in the morning, you two?
C: Er...
M: Later than you.
C: Yes! I get up er, oh, well, **(15) I tend to get up about 8**...
I: Mmm, hmm.
C: ...7 o'clock in the morning.
I: Is that 'cos you can't sleep, or...
C: Er, no. I can, I could sleep. (laughs)
I: (laughs)
C: I could sleep for a very long time. (laughs)
I: Right.
C: Er, no, that's normally because I start... There's a lot of days at the moment where I'm starting work at 9 or 10 in the morning.
I: Mmm.
C: So...

A Typical Day

I: And you have to get **(16) the Tube** into work?
C: Yeah, and that's, **(17) that's a hassle**, especially at that time in the morning. Always add an extra half an hour.
I: 'Cos of **(18) the rush hour**.
C: Yeah. (*laughs*) It's not very rushing, really.
I: So, so you're going in earlier than Martin is, presumably.
C: Yeah.
I: Right.
M: Yeah.
I: So what time do you get up in the morning normally?
M: I'll normally get up . . . er, depending on what time I'm supposed to be in, but normally around 10.
I: Mmm.
M: Um, anywhere between 9 and 10 on an early day. Sometimes, if I've worked later the night before, um, and I don't need to be in till much later, then I'll leave it until about midday or one o'clock.
I: To get up?
M: To get up.
I: (laughs)
C: **(19) He's lazy!**
M: I like my sleep! (*laughs*)
I: Yes, I do, too. So you don't have breakfast together.
C: No.
M: No.
I: Do you get . . . And you can't have lunch together 'cos you're working . . .
C: Well, sometimes . . . It depends on what day it is. Um, if Martin's in for, for like 10 o'clock in the morning and I'm at the Opera House and we're doing two shows, or we're doing **(20) a rehearsal**, um, we have to finish at about three-th . . . um, **(21) the cut-off time is about 2.30**, so I get **(22) an hour's break** then. And sometimes that's when Martin's available to go out for a dinner, so sometimes we meet up between shows, but not . . . obviously not on a Thursday . . .
M: Yeah.
C: . . . but on a day where he's got a rehearsal.
I: Mmm, hmm.
C: And then the other time is on a Friday, isn't it, where you come over to the Opera House and he comes up to **(23) the canteen** with me um, because you've normally finished doing **(24) your maintenance** in the . . . Friday in daytime . . .
M: Yes.
C: . . . in time for me to have dinner.
M: I'm normally done by about half-five . . .
C: Yeah.
M: . . . which is when you go on a break.

C: Before the show, and I don't have to be back for the show till about 7 o'clock, so we've got about an hour to spend with each other and we eat dinner together.
I: Oh, that's nice. In, in central London.
C: In central . . . We go to the Opera House canteen 'cos it's . . . we get served there quickly 'cos it's obviously . . .
M: Yes.
C: . . . **(25) in-house**.
M: And it's nice and relaxing and it has a lovely view.
C: Yes. Beautiful view. Beautiful view.
I: What of?
C: Um, you can see Battersea Power Station from there.
I: Uh, huh.
C: And the London Eye. Er, you can see Parliament er . . .
M: Yeah. Well, Big Ben.
C: Oh, Big Ben, yeah, and . . .
M: And it overlooks **(26) the Piazza of Cov** . . . Covent Garden.
C: Covent Garden.
I: Oh, right.
C: Beautiful - it's one of the best views.
I: So how , how far does it . . . How long does it take you to walk to Caroline's . . . to the Royal Opera House?
M: About five minutes.
C: Mmm.
I: Oh, that's great.
M: From Leicester, Leicester Square to Covent Garden um . . . Through the back roads it's about five minutes. It's . . . It'd be longer if you take the main road, but I think it's only about 10 minutes, though, that way.
C: **(27) It depends how crowded it is as well.**
M: Yes.
C: On Saturday it takes like twice that amount of time because people are slow and want to go shopping. (*laughs*)
M: And don't move!
I: (*Laughs*) And they say in London it's all short **(28) steps** and long steps, isn't it?
C: Yes.
I: Um, so at, at night you meet up . . .
C: Yes.
I: . . . together, after every show.
C: Yes. And we go home together.
I: On the Tube.
C: Yeah.
M: Yes.
I: OK. So what time are you back here in Walthamstow?
C: About 11.
M: Yeah.

UNIT 8: *Caroline and Martin* **109**

C: Norm . . . usually. If we, **(29) if our shows come down about five past 10, quarter past 10** um, **(30) we normally make it back to Walthamstow for about 11 o'clock.** Um . . .
I: So when you come home er, on a work day, what, what do you do?
C: Go home, watch the "Family Guy."
M: Yeah.
I: Watch the what? I didn't . . .
M: Watch . . .
C: "Family Guy."
M: Er . . .
C: The **(31) cartoon.**
I: Oh, that's your favourite programme?
C: Yeah, yeah. We've got, so we've recorded so much of it. It's on every night so we, we record it every night. So we go home, watch that. Sometimes have a pint at the pub . . .
I: OK.
C: . . . and . . .
M: Um, feed the cats.
C: Feed the cats, yeah, and then go to bed. (*laughs*)
I: So weekends, are you free at the weekends?
C: **(32) Barely.**
M: No.
C: No, you're not any more. Um . . .
M: No, not at all.
I: I'm normally free on a Sunday. That's normally my day off.
I: Right.

C: **(33) Or recovering from doing an overnight shift.**
I: An overnight shift?
C: Saturday night. Yes.
I: So you have work . . .
C: Overnight?
I: . . . all through the night.
C: All through the night.
I: What time do you start?
C: Um, well **(34) last Saturday it was fun.** I started at 10 o'clock in the morning – Saturday morning. Um, and then I worked through till half-past two.
I: Right.
C: Um. Then I had a three-hour break um, and then I went down into the studio theatre at the Opera House, started there at 5pm, finished the show at half-past 10 and then we had to take **(35) the set** down and put it in a um, in a lorry er, and we didn't get out of there . . . didn't get home until 7 o'clock in the morning. So I couldn't sleep because **(36) you're buzzing at the end of a night like that.**
I: So you worked 20 hours, or more.
C: Yeah.
I: Gosh!
C: I wasn't awake for all 20 hours! I did fall asleep between shifts. (*laughs*)
I: OK.
C: **(37) Grab sleep where you can.** (*laughs*)

7. Words and Phrases

1. Leicester – a city in the East Midlands of England
2. performances – entertainments such as plays, ballets, and opera
3. I guess – I assume
4. ridiculously long days – stupidly/unreasonably long working days
5. Did you get overtime for that? – Did you get paid extra money for that?
6. a set contract – a fixed contract, i.e., the number of hours per working week were fixed
7. a set salary – a fixed amount of money paid for each month's work, regardless of the hours
8. the scenery backstage – the painted pictures on backdrops on a stage used to represent where the action is taking place
9. the Royal Opera House in Covent Garden – An historic building which is home of the Royal Opera, the Royal Ballet, and the Orchestra of the Royal Opera House. Covent Garden is an area in central London full of theatres, street performers, and interesting shops.
10. the studio theatre – a small experimental theatre – not the main theatre
11. It varies through the week. – It changes during the week.
12. without fail – always
13. the hours have shifted much more toward eve . . . the evenings – Martin now tends to work later hours than before.
14. It depends on, on what I'm supposed to be doing. – It varies according to what I have to do.
15. I tend to get up about 8 – I usually get up at around 8
16. the Tube – the colloquial name of the London Underground train system
17. that's a hassle – something which causes difficulties or stress
18. the rush hour – the busy time of day when lots of people are travelling to, or from, work
19. He's lazy! – (in this case) He prefers to stay in bed and do nothing than get up.
20. a rehearsal – a time when the people involved in a play, ballet, opera, etc. practise before they give their first official opening performance
21. the cut-off time is about 2.30 – the time we have to stop work is around 2.30
22. an hour's break – an hour free from work
23. the canteen – a place in a factory or other place of work where the employees can buy food or drink, generally at lower prices
24. your maintenance – the work Martin does to keep the lights, etc. in good working order
25. in-house – The canteen is only available to people who work at the Royal Opera House.
26. the Piazza of Covent Garden – the open area of Covent Garden which is often used by street performers hoping to make money
27. It depends how crowded it is as well. – It depends on how many people are there – it takes longer to walk if there are lots of people in the streets.
28. steps – you take steps one after the other when you walk
29. if our shows come down about five past 10 – If our shows finish around five past 10
30. we normally make it back to Walthamstow for 11 o'clock – we normally manage to get back to Walthamstow at 11 o'clock
31. (a) cartoon – a programme or film made using drawings or computer-generated images (CGI)
32. Barely. – Hardly ever.
33. Or recovering from doing an overnight shift. – Or getting back to normal again after working all night.
34. last Saturday it was fun – Here Caroline is being sarcastic. She didn't really have a good time.
35. the set – the scenery on the stage, i.e., the painted backdrops
36. you're buzzing at the end of a night like that – you can't relax because your head is spinning
37. Grab sleep where you can. – Try to take the chance to have a sleep whenever you can.

UNIT 9 Anne

1. Pre-Listening Comprehension

A Schema building

Anne comes from the Midlands in the heart of England. She and her husband recently moved to the Greek island of Crete, where Anne works as a holiday rep. How much do you know about Greece and Crete? Discuss the following statements with a partner and mark them True or False.

1. T F Greece has over 1400 islands, the largest of which is Crete.
2. T F Crete is the largest island in the Mediterranean.
3. T F Crete was the capital of the Minoan civilisation (2,600 – 1,400 BC) – the oldest European civilisation.
4. T F The traditional Greek speciality, feta cheese, is white and sweet.

A Typical Day

B Discussion

Discuss the questions in small groups. Share your answers with the class.

1. How many holiday-related words can you think of?
2. Have you ever been to Greece or Crete on holiday? What do people do there on holiday?
3. What are some reasons Anne and her husband might have decided to move from England to Crete?
4. What are some of the things a holiday rep might have to do in a typical day?

C Normalisation

This exercise is designed to help you get used to Anne's voice. Listen to the first part of the interview and answer the questions.

1. When does Anne normally start work?
2. How many properties is she looking after at the moment?
3. How long does she spend in each property?

Crete

2. Listening Comprehension

A Gap-Fill
🎧 161

In this first exercise Anne talks about a typical working day. Before you listen, try to predict which words, or which **types** of words will fit in the gaps. Then listen and check your answers.

1. Basically _____ there if anybody _____ you or _____ you.
2. There may be some _____ that you have to _____ with.
3. Sometimes people just want to _____.
4. They want to tell Anne what _____ ___ been _____.
5. Anne also liaises with the hotel _____.
6. Anne has a _____ in the _____ of the day before returning in the _____ and doing the same _____.
7. Sometimes Anne takes _____ for excursions and deals with any _____ people have with their_____, etc.
8. For example sometimes people are _____ over a _____ and they want to _____.

B Sentence completion
🎧 162

Anne talks about getting people to and from the airport. As with Exercise A, before you listen, try to predict which words, or which types of words will fit in the gaps. Then listen and check your answers.

1. Next Anne talks about _____ _____ _____.
2. She's told where she will be _____ _____.
3. She turns up and collects the _____.
4. She then takes people _____ _____ _____.
5. She makes sure they're _____ _____ _____.
6. She then waits for the flight she's been given to _____ _____.
7. She makes sure people are dropped off at _____ _____ _____.
8. On a Friday Anne begins work at _____.
9. She then finishes at about eight _____ _____ _____ _____.

114   *A Typical Day*

C True/False

Anne talks about the day after she collects new guests. Listen and decide if each statement is True (T) or False (F). Remember to give reasons for your answers.

1. T F Sometimes Anne has to work all night.
2. T F People always have a welcome meeting the day they arrive.
3. T F If Anne works through the night on a Friday, she has the afternoon and evening free.
4. T F On these days she usually stays at home for the rest of the day.
5. T F Welcome meetings generally take place just after breakfast.

3. Features of a Midlands Accent

A Pronunciation –
cup /ʌ/ and put /ʊ/

(164)

Like many native speakers in northern England and the Midlands, Anne does not distinguish the vowel sound found in the word *cup* in standard English from the vowel sound found in *put*.

Listen to how first Anne, and then your teacher, pronounce the following excerpts. Can you hear the differences?

> a normal day would be um, <u>coming</u> in in the morning
> and then <u>come</u> back again in the evening
> I'm given details of where I'm going to get picked <u>up</u>
> There's not really a typical day, as <u>such</u>.
> But then, as soon as I've finished at <u>lunchtime</u>
> and then be ready for sort of a midnight <u>pick-up</u>

B The glottal stop

(165)

The glottal stop (i.e. not pronouncing fully the *-t* sound at the end of words such as *got* or *lot*, or the *-t-* sounds in words such as *bottle* or *kettle*) is a common feature of many British accents, and is used particularly by younger people.

Underline where Anne uses a glottal stop in the following excerpts:

1. *and spending about an hour in each property*
2. *you li . . . liaise with the hotel owners as well, if they've er, got any queries*
3. *deal with any problems that people have got with rooms*
4. *they don't like it and they ask to move*
5. *and then take people to the airport*

116 *A Typical Day*

4. Further Language Development

A Extension exercise

Fill in the blanks in these new sentences with words you heard during Anne's interview. The words are listed in the box to help you.

> bed   break   chat   complaints   doing
> dropped   excursions   flight   liaise   off   owners
> picked   properties   ready   right   spending

1. Aren't you _____ yet? It's nearly half-past and I said we'd be there at eight.
2. You're _____ a lot of time in the library these days. What's up? Are you in love with the librarian or something?
3. After we _____ Marco off at his place, we drove back to my place and had a coffee.
4. The customer services manager is responsible for dealing with _____ from customers.
5. I think there should be a special tax for dog _____ to pay for pavement cleaning.
6. Why don't you go to _____? You look exhausted.
7. Julie's the richest person I know. She owns _____ all over London. She buys places that need a lot of work, gets the work done, and then sells them on at a huge profit.
8. I think you should have a _____ now. You've been sitting at that computer for hours.
9. She said she needed to see me urgently, but then it turned out she just wanted to _____ about her new boyfriend.
10. My job is to _____ between the customers and the suppliers, so I spend most of my time on the phone.
11. When we went to Malaga we went on _____ every other day; otherwise it just gets too boring, lying on the beach all day.
12. What have you been _____ since we last met?
13. Stefan _____ me up in his car at 7 and then we drove to Lansdowne Park and met the others there.

UNIT 9: Anne 117

14. Do you know your _____ number? Once we've got that we can find out where you need to check in.
15. Are you sure you've got the _____ number? This is 020 8523 6592.
16. Are you doing anything special next Friday? It's just I've got the day _____ and I thought it'd be nice if we could do something together.

B Transformations

Change the word in each bracket which Anne used in her interview to form a word which fits the gap:

1. I don't (normal) _____ go out on Friday evening. I just have a quiet night in.
2. We (spending) _____ most of our holiday decorating our spare bedroom, so I was exhausted when I went back to work.
3. Do stop (complaints) _____ !
4. Have you (telling) _____ your mother what happened at school today?
5. My grandparents (owners) _____ a sweetshop when we were little, so that was perfect.
6. I've (bookings) _____ tickets for that new musical for Yuko's birthday.
7. What's the (situated) _____ with Markus and Helga? Are they back together again?
8. She gave me very (details) _____ instructions on how to get there, but we still got lost.
9. We often go out (picked) _____ mushrooms in the woods in the autumn.
10. What time do we need to (checked) _____ in?
11. What's the (different) _____ between a Kiwi fruit and a Chinese gooseberry?
12. What's your estimated time of (arrive) _____ ?
13. When we used to live in London we always got a lot of (visit) _____ .
14. We'll be there soon! We're just (finished) _____ dinner.
15. Have you two (meetings) _____ yet?

118   *A Typical Day*

C Phrasal Verbs

Insert the following phrasal verbs taken from Anne's interview into the gaps:

> check in   deal with   drop off
> look after   pick up   turn up

1. Can you _____ _____ my handbag while I go the restroom?
2. We'll _____ you _____ at 7, if that's OK.
3. I have to _____ _____ a lot of angry people in my line of work because I'm a complaints manager.
4. We've invited about 50 people, but we only expect about 30 of them to _____ _____.
5. You normally have to _____ _____ at least an hour before your flight.
6. Is it OK if I _____ you _____ here as the traffic's so bad? It'll probably be quicker for you to walk.

UNIT 9: *Anne*   119

5. Transcript

I: Interviewer **A:** Anne (2'37")

I: OK, Anne, can you tell me about a typical day as **(1) a holiday rep**?

A: OK. Um, a, a normal day would be um, coming in in the morning. Um, I look after three different **(2) properties** at this time of year um, and spending about an hour in each property. Um, basically you're there if anybody needs you or wants you. Um, you may have some complaints um, that you have **(3) to deal with**, or it may just be people wanting **(4) to chat**, telling you what they've been doing, that type of thing. Um, you li ... **(5) liaise with** the hotel owners as well, if they've er, got any **(6) queries**, that type of thing. Um, and I do that for sort of an hour in each property. Then I would have **(7) a break** in the middle of the day, free time, and then come back again in the evening and do the same thing in the evening. Um, you know, I may take bookings for **(8) excursions** during that time um, deal with any problems that people have got with rooms, and that type of thing. Some people are situated perhaps over a bar and then they don't like it and they ask to move and ... so that type of thing. That's a normal day. We do have airport duty days where I'm um, I'm given details of **(9) where I'm going to get picked up** and **(10) I turn up** and collect the coach and then take people to the airport um, see that they're checked in OK, wait for the, the flight that I've been given to bring back and **(11) make sure people are dropped off at er, at the right places** as well. Um, they can be odd days er, Friday here, um, that all starts about midnight and goes through about, till about eight o'clock in the morning, so that ... It, it ... There's not really a typical day, as such, there are all different times.

I: OK. So sometimes you're working all through the night, then.

A: Yeah, yeah.

I: Would you get the next day off?

A: No, you never have the next day off 'cos the, the day that people arrive, the next day is welcome meeting day and that's a really big day for us. What you would have, if I worked through the night on a Friday, I'd visit my ... **(12) do my duties**, visit the hotels in the morning, but then as soon as I've finished at lunchtime, I have the afternoon and evening off, so that's when I would go to bed ...

I: Mmm, hmm.

A: ... visit the beach, that sort of thing, and then be ready for sort of a midnight pick-up. But the next day um, I usually schedule welcome meetings um, to start around lunchtime, so you've got the next morning off to get some sleep. (*laughs*)

A Typical Day

6. Words and Phrases

1. **a holiday rep** – a person who works for a holiday company
2. **properties** – buildings (NB in this case hotels)
3. **to deal with** – to handle, to resolve
4. **to chat** – to talk informally with someone about things that are not very important just for the pleasure of talking
5. **liaise with** – to exchange information with people so that things work well
6. **queries** – questions asked to find out information or to check that the information you have is correct
7. **a break** – a period of time when you stop what you are doing to rest
8. **excursions** – trips organised for groups of people, especially for people on holiday
9. **where I'm going to get picked up** – where the coach is going to stop and collect her
10. **I turn up** – an informal way of say 'I arrived' as in 'He'd been waiting since 8, but I didn't turn up till half-past because the traffic was so bad.'
11. **make sure people are dropped off at the right places** – make sure people are taken to the correct hotels
12. **do my duties** – do the various things I have to do as part of my job

UNIT 10 Fernand

1. Pre-Listening Comprehension

A Schema building

Fernand comes from a Flemish town in Belgium. Fernand is a *sommelier*, i.e. a trained expert in wines. At the moment he is working at a private gentleman's club in central London which operates as a hotel, lounge and restaurant. How much do you know about Belgium? Discuss the following statements with a partner and mark them True or False.

1. T F The Belgians claim they invented *frites*, or French fries.
2. T F Brussels is the headquarters of both NATO and the United Nations.
3. T F Antwerp is the gold capital of the world.
4. T F Belgium is also famous for beer, moules (mussels), waffles and chocolate.

A Typical Day

B **Discussion**

Discuss the questions in small groups. Share your answers with the class.

1. Do you know anything else about Belgium?
2. What do you think are the main responsibilities of someone working in a private gentleman's club?
3. Why do you think Fernand moved to the UK from Belgium?

C **Normalisation**

167

This exercise is designed to help you get used to Fernand's voice. Listen to the first part of the interview and answer the questions.

1. What time does Fernand wake up when he's doing an early shift?
2. Where does he take the Victoria line to?
3. What time does he have breakfast?
4. What kind of eggs does he sometimes have for breakfast?

UNIT 10: *Ferdinand*

2. Listening Comprehension

A Questions

🎧 168

In this initial exercise Fernand talks about his mornings at work. Listen and answer the questions.

1. Who does Fernand have to get the club ready for?
2. What do people like to read at the club?
3. What do people sometimes ask Fernand about?

B Multiple choice

🎧 169

Fernand talks about lunch at work. Listen and choose a, b or c.

Fernand . . . a. eats lunch with the members in the dining room.
b. shares the food he brings in with his colleagues.
c. eats the same food as the members of the club.

C Gap-fill

🎧 170

Fernand talks about his different shifts. Before you listen, try to predict which words, or which **types** of words will fit in the gaps. Then listen and check your answers.

1. If Fernand does an early shift, he finishes work at _____ pm.
2. If he does a late session, he gets a free _____ with the rest of the _____.
3. A late shift ends at _____ pm.
4. Fernand used to be a _____ waiter.
5. When he's doing a late shift, Fernand gets up at _____ o'clock at the _____.
6. He makes his own _____ at home.
7. On a late shift he starts work at around _____ to _____.

124 *A Typical Day*

D True/False

🎧 171

Fernand talks about his afternoons and evenings. Listen and decide if each statement is True (T) or False (F). Remember to give reasons for your answers.

1. T F The nearest Tube station to Fernand's club is Green Park.
2. T F His friend lives a few minutes' walk from the club.
3. T F His friend has serious health problems.
4. T F She lives in her own house.
5. T F After a late shift, Fernand usually travels back to Walthamstow.
6. T F He's generally so tired when he comes home after a late shift that he goes straight to bed.
7. T F Sometimes he goes to a pub called The Old Wick.
8. T F Occasionally he eats out.

3. Interesting Language Points

A Features of a Flemish accent – The *th* sound

🎧 172

The letters *th* found at the start of words such as *the* and *think* are difficult for Flemish speakers, and many non-native English speakers, to pronounce. Often they use the letter *d* for the *th* sound in *the* and *this* and *t* for the *th* sound found in *think* and *things*.

Part 1
At the beginning of Fernand's interview his pronunciation is extremely good, but as the interview goes on he begins to say *dis* and *tree* more and more. Listen to the way he substitutes *d* for *th* in the following extracts:

> So <u>then</u> I continue to do <u>the</u>, <u>the</u> morning shift . . .
> and <u>that</u> everything's ready for <u>them</u>
> I also help <u>them</u>
> <u>then</u> we do a split shift

Part 2
🎧 173

Now listen to how Fernand substitutes *t* for *th* in the following extracts:

> still following up <u>everything</u> what's [sic – that's] happening
> I finish around <u>three</u> o'clock

Part 3
🎧 174

In the following sentences Fernand uses both *d* and *t* for the *th* sound:

> preparing <u>everything</u> for <u>the</u> members to arrive
> we finish up <u>the</u> session at <u>three</u> o'clock
> <u>That</u> is <u>the</u> normal life.

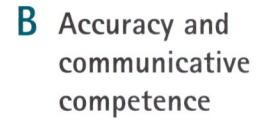

B Accuracy and communicative competence

Although Fernand speaks very good English, he does make a number of grammatical errors. However, these do not affect comprehension – it is still clear to the listener what he is talking about. Can you make the following excerpts from the interview more accurate?

1. *I have a breakfast at work which is typical English.*
2. *very fresh prepared*
3. *I normally always go up at the latest 8 o'clock.*
4. *I have then my own breakfast which consists on bread and marmalade.*
5. *I come straight to here.* [i.e. home]
6. *I read English books also.*

4. Further Language Development

A Extension exercise

Fill in the blanks in these new sentences with words you heard during Fernand's interview. The words are listed in the box to help you.

> accommodation   depending   disabled   dressed   feel
> mood   place   scrambled   share   shift
> shopping   straight   trimmings   typical   wake

1. Generally, _____ on the weather, I either take the tram or walk to work.
2. What time would you like me to get to your _____?
3. We normally do our food _____ on a Monday evening, because the supermarket is really quiet then.
4. Do you _____ like going out tonight? Or shall we have a quiet night in?
5. I was making _____ eggs for breakfast, but then the phone rang and I left the saucepan on, so now I need a new one.
6. We had a wonderful Sunday lunch – roast beef with all the _____.
7. The most difficult thing about living here is finding cheap _____.
8. It was dark when I got _____ this morning and it was only when I got to work that I saw I was wearing one blue sock and one black one.
9. I'm on the late _____ this week so I don't start work till 3.
10. My neighbour is _____ so I give him a hand with his garden sometimes.
11. After work I usually come _____ home, except on a Wednesday when I go to the gym.
12. It's just _____ of Kurt to be late.
13. The boss is in a really good _____ today, for a change.
14. I'm not very hungry, so we could just _____ a starter if you like.
15. I usually _____ up at about 7, even at the weekend.

B Transformations

Change the word in each bracket which Fernand used in his interview to form a word which fits the gap.

1. The (early) _____ you get there, the better.
2. I can only write on (line) _____ paper.
3. I do like Jan, but he can be a bit (mood) _____ at times.
4. When you're cooking a big dinner, the (prepared) _____ is very important.
5. Which motoring (organise) _____ does she work for? Is it the AA?
6. The best person to ask is Claire. She's always very (help) _____.
7. My partner is a (profession) _____ artist.
8. We weren't very hungry so we just (share) _____ a pizza.
9. I've been feeling a bit tired (late) _____. Perhaps I should go to the doctor.
10. We're very short-(staff) _____ at the moment because so many people are off work with 'flu.
11. What's the (heavy) _____ metal? It's lead, isn't it?
12. Can you children play a bit more (quiet) _____? I can't hear myself think!
13. Which is the (near) _____ Tube station to where you work? Is it Marble Arch or Bond Street?
14. Hospital patients are normally only allowed two (visit) _____ at a time.
15. Tanya's new boyfriend isn't very (friend) _____, is he?
16. Have you (speak) _____ to your parents yet about us going on holiday together?
17. How are you (feel) _____?
18. Please take a (seating) _____.
19. Patients are generally very well (information) _____ when they come in for an operation.
20. Can you ask the (waiting) _____ to come over?

A Typical Day

5. Transcript 🎧 175 I: Interviewer   F: Fernand   (4'36")

I: Can you tell me about a typical day?
F: Yeah. Depending on (1) **the shift** I'm working – if I'm doing an early shift and all that I'll wake up about er, five, five-thirty. Take my shower. Er, get dressed, of course, (2) **otherwise they'll arrest me**. Er, take (3) **the Victoria line** and go to (4) **Green Park** and go to work and start opening (5) **the session** for the day. At 8 o'clock then I have a breakfast at work which is typical English, sometimes French because we have er, some days (6) **croissants**. And sometimes when er, the morning (7) **chef** is (8) **in a good mood** or not we have some (9) **scrambled eggs**.
I: Hmm.
F: (10) **Not with all the, all the trimmings**, but er, and they're nice.
I: Mmm, hmm.
F: Very fresh prepared. So then I continue to do the, the morning shift, preparing everything for the members to arrive.
I: Mmm.
F: Organise [sic – Make sure that] that the members are er, welcome and that everything's ready for them i.e. newspapers, magazines and er, seating. And also that when they need information that we can provide them. I also help them when, if they come in or when they come in and ask me about the wines and all that I can help them out because of my profession, which is normally er, (11) **head sommelier**. At er, lunch we have then er, the facility to share, although not in the same room, but er, (12) **we can share**, so the menu, the buffet menu, with the members.
I: Mmm, hmm.
F: And then afterwards er, we fini . . . I finish up, or we finish up the session at 3 o'clock.
I: OK.
F: If we do a late session then we also have a dinner, which is a staff dinner, and er, we finish at 9 o'clock in the evening.
I: Hmm.
F: When I'm doing, when I was doing . . . or when I will do again, the, the wine waiting system then we do (13) **a split shift**. And then we have a lunch break and we have a dinner break.
I: OK.
F: That is the normal life.
I: Mmm, hmm. When you're doing a late shift, what time do you get up?
F: When I'm doing late shift I normally always go up [sic – get up] at the latest 8 o'clock.
I: Mmm, hmm.
F: I have then my own breakfast which er, consists on [sic – of] bread and (14) **marmalade** because I don't believe too much and too heavy in the morning.
I: Right.
F: I go to, go to work, have my lunch er... start about 12, half-past twelve, have my lunch round er, 1 o'clock and then er, do the quiet afternoon shift, but still following up everything what's [sic – that's] happening . . .
I: OK.
F: . . . at the club.
I: Right. So er, after you finish work, if you're on an ear . . . early shift you finish work at 3, I think?
F: Yeah.
I: Yeah. What do you do then? Because you're right . . . Which Tube station are you near with the club?
F: I'm near to Green Park but what I do then, I'm going to, and this is not to make er, my name and all that, but I go to visit a friend. I finish around 3 o'clock, I arrive at her place around quarter to 4, 4 o'clock, and (15) **she's disabled for life**.
I: Mmm, hmm.
F: I go visit her and I do her shopping and sit with her, listen to her, and speak with her and, and that's it. She lives in er, in temporary accommodation.
I: OK. Mmm, hmm. So you do that when you finish early. What about when you finish at 9 o'clock? (16) **'Cos** that's quite late.
F: Nine o'clock I come straight to here. (Sic – I come straight back home.)
I: Yeah. OK. Straight home.
F: Yeah, and go to bed after reading a few books, or rather a few pages in a book and all that, I go to bed.
I: OK. Do you read English books?
F: Yeah, I read English books also, yeah.
I: Do, do you ever go out at, at night?
F: Sometimes, yes. Er, (17) **when I feel like it**, and all that, well, I go to er, to (18) **the local pubs**, one of them being the, the Old Vic. The other one before, I don't go any more, I don't go that much anymore, was the Soul, which was a wine bar.
I: Mmm, hmm.
F: And er, sometimes er, if I feel like it, I might go out to a Turkish er, kebab shop or some pleasant Chinese . . .
I: OK.

UNIT 10: *Ferdinand* **129**

6. Words and Phrases

1. **the shift** – The period of time during the day that Fernand works. The early shift is from around 7am to 3pm and the late shift is from 12 noon to 9pm.
2. **otherwise they'll arrest me** – Here Fernand is making a joke. He says that if he doesn't get dressed before leaving the house the police will take him to a police station and question him.
3. **the Victoria line** – The Underground line (light blue on the Tube map) which goes from Walthamstow in north-east London to Brixton in south London.
4. **Green Park** – an area of central London near Piccadilly
5. **the session** – the club has a morning session and an afternoon/evening session
6. **croissants** – pieces of light crescent-shaped pastry usually eaten at breakfast, particularly in France
7. **chef** – a trained cook
8. **in a good mood** – If you are in a good mood you feel cheerful and good about life
9. **scrambled** – eggs mixed with a little milk or cream which are stirred while they are cooking
10. **Not with all the trimmings** – A full English breakfast 'with all the trimmings' consists of bacon, egg, tomatoes, mushrooms, fried bread, black pudding, etc. Likewise 'roast lamb with all the trimmings' would consist of lamb, vegetables and mint sauce. The 'trimmings' are all the separate food items that come with the main dish.
11. **head sommelier** – the chief wine waiter
12. **we can share the buffet menu with the members** – A buffet is a meal where people serve themselves from the various dishes of food on offer. Fernand eats the same food as the members, but not in the same room.
13. **a split shift** – two periods of work on the same day with a break in the middle
14. **marmalade** – a soft substance like jam which is made from citrus fruit such as oranges, lemons, limes and grapefruit
15. **she's disabled for life** – She has severe physical problems which she will not recover from
16. **'Cos** – short for 'because'
17. **when I feel like it** – when I want to do this
18. **the local pubs** – the bars in the area where Fernand lives

A Typical Day

A Place I Know Well

UNIT 11 Scott

1. Pre-Listening Comprehension

A Schema building

We heard Scott talking about his family in Unit 3. Scott is a 23-year-old man from Australia. How much do you know about Australia? Circle the correct answer.

1. Australia is the **fourth / fifth / sixth** largest nation in the world.

2. About **30 / 50 / 70** percent of the population of Australia live in the country's 10 largest cities, mainly on the eastern seaboard and in the south-eastern corner.

3. Residents of Australia born overseas make up about **one quarter / one half / two thirds** of the population.

4. The capital of Australia is **Canberra / Sydney / Adelaide**.

B Discussion

Discuss the questions in small groups. Share your answers with the class.

1. Do you know anything else about Australia?
2. Why do you think Scott decided to leave Australia and go to live in London?
3. Do you know what an Australian accent sounds like?

C Normalisation

(176)

This exercise is designed to help you get used to Scott's voice. Before you listen, try to predict which words, or which types of words (nouns, adjectives, prepositions, parts of verbs, etc.) will fit in the gaps. Then listen and check your answers.

1. Maida Vale is _____ _____ from Regent's Park.
2. Scott _____ to Maida Vale just over a _____ ago.
3. He says Maida Vale is _____ a _____ nice part of London.
4. It's very _____.
5. The _____ are very wide.
6. _____ lives in mansionettes.
7. When you _____ down the _____, every house _____ exactly the same.
8. Mansionettes are something the _____ are keen on, according to Scott.
9. A mansionette is _____ a block of two- or three-_____ _____.
10. Scott's address is _____ Elgin Mansions and there is another _____ next _____ called Biddulph Mansions.

Regent's Park

UNIT 11: *Scott* 133

2. Listening Comprehension

A Questions
(177)

In this first exercise, Scott talks about Maida Vale and the apartment he shares. Listen and answer the questions.

1. What are mansion blocks in Maida Vale made from?
2. What is Maida Vale full of?
3. How many people live in Scott's apartment altogether?
4. Describe them:
   _____
5. How many single and double bedrooms are there?
6. Which rooms do Scott and his flatmates share?
7. Why do young people in London tend to share flats?

B Gap-Fill
(178)

Scott talks some more about flat-sharing. Before you listen, try to predict which words, or which **types** of words (nouns, adjectives, prepositions, parts of verbs, etc.) will fit in the gaps. Then listen and check your answers.

1. Scott says he's quite _____ because he and his flatmates _____ on well.
2. They live like a _____.
3. They _____ the cooking.
4. When Scott first _____ to London he wanted to live somewhere a bit _____.
5. At one time he was _____ with up to _____ people.

C Questions
(179)

Scott talks about his previous accommodation. Listen and answer the questions.

1. Which countries did Scott's flatmates in his first flat come from?
2. In which part of London was Scott's first flatshare?

A Place I Know Well

D Gap-Fill

180

Scott talks about how happy he is living in Maida Vale. As with Exercise B, try to predict which words, or which **types** of words (nouns, adjectives, prepositions, parts of verbs, etc.) will fit in the gaps. Then listen and check your answers.

1. Scott says it was great _____ sharing with lots of people, but it got a bit much after a _____.
2. Scott says where he lives now is _____ _____ to his first flatshare.
3. He isn't _____ to move any time _____.
4. Scott says he certainly _____ _____ to buy a house in Maida Vale.
5. Another word for rich is '_____'.
6. Maida Vale is quite near St. _____ _____, which is _____ distance to Lords cricket ground.
7. Scott is a cricket _____.

E Questions

181

Scott talks about making the most of where you live. Listen and answer the questions.

1. Which other area is Maida Vale close to?
2. What does London have a lot of?
3. When does Scott like walking from Maida Vale to Regent's Park and Camden Town?
4. Where did Scott move to Maida Vale from?
5. Which water sport did Scott take up when he lived there?
6. Where did he use to go running?

F Gap-Fill

182

Scott talks about exercise. As with Exercises B and D, try to predict which words, or which **types** of words, will fit in the gaps. Then listen and check your answers.

1. The interviewer asks if Scott is _____ down as he gets _____.
2. She points out that before moving to Maida Vale, Scott used to go _____ along the _____.
3. Now he spends his free time _____ along the canal bank and _____ cricket.
4. Scott admits he is doing less _____ than he was two years ago.

3. Interesting Language Points

A Using the present simple and the present continuous

We generally use the present simple to talk about facts and things that happen regularly. Look at how Scott uses the present simple in the following excerpts from the interview:

> At the moment I <u>live</u> in Maida Vale.
> Everyone <u>lives</u> in mansionettes, so you <u>walk</u> down the street and every house <u>looks</u> exactly the same.

We generally use the present continuous when we are talking about things that are happening at the moment, as in these excerpts:

> <u>I'm not planning</u> to move any time soon.
> Do you think <u>you're slowing down</u> as <u>you're getting</u> older?
> Now <u>you're walking</u> along canal banks...
> <u>I'm certainly doing</u> less exercise than I was two years ago...

B Using the simple past and the past continuous

We use the simple past to talk about completed actions in the past. We often use the simple past with a time expression, as in this excerpt:

> I <u>moved</u> there about a year... a bit over a year ago.

We use the past continuous when we are talking about an action which continued for some time in the past, as in this example:

> 'This time last year I <u>was living</u> in Tokyo.'

We often use the simple past and the past continuous together to indicate that a longer action was interrupted by a shorter action:

> 'I <u>was having</u> a bath when you <u>called</u>, that's why it went to voicemail.'
> 'We <u>were walking</u> home last night when suddenly it <u>started</u> to snow.'

Now look at how Scott and the interviewer use the past continuous in these excerpts from the interview:

> When I first <u>got</u> to London, obviously I <u>was looking</u> for something a bit cheaper.
> Well, first you <u>were jogging</u> and things on the river. Now you're walking along canal banks...

C The Australian accent and the letter *i*

🎧 183

Australian native speakers tend to pronounce the letter *i* with more rounded lips and a more curled tongue than British native speakers so that it almost sounds like the letter *o* is followed by the letter *i*, as in the word *toy*. Listen to how Scott pronounces the letter *i* in the following excerpts:

1. *very... um, **wide** streets*
2. *It's certainly a term **I** wasn't familiar with until I came to London.*
3. *I'm certainly doing less **exercise** than I was two years ago.*

D The Australian accent and rising intonation

🎧 184

Australian native speakers often use rising intonation for statements when British native speakers would use falling intonation, although nowadays many young British native speakers also use rising intonation for statements. Listen to how Scott pronounces these excerpts from the interview:

1. *at the moment I live in Maida Vale*
2. *there's particularly a lot of rich, rich houses there*
3. *it's also close to an area called Little Venice*

Regent's Canal

4. Further Listening Practice

A Recognising sentence stress

🎧 185

Stressed words are the most important in spoken English because they carry the most meaning. Which words do you think Scott stresses in the following extracts? Underline them. Then listen to check your answers.

1. It's certainly a term I wasn't familiar with until I came to London
2. so my address is 96 Elgin Mansions
3. Maida Vale is full of three or four-bed... three or two-bedroom apartments, basically.
4. I live in a three-bedroom one.
5. there's a couple in the main room
6. we share the living room and we share kitchen and we share bathroom
7. But er, when I first got to London obviously I was looking for something a bit cheaper, even then.
8. I certainly couldn't afford to buy a house there.
9. So yeah, it is quite a, quite an affluent area.
10. I'm certainly doing less exercise than I was two years ago.

B Linking

Linking occurs when the end of one word runs_into the start_of the next word. It is very common in informal spoken English, but less so in more formal English, such as speeches or lectures.

The most common linking occurs between the letter *–s* at the end of a word when the next word begins with a vowel, as in these excerpts from the interview:

🎧 186

1. *Everyone lives_in mansionettes.*
2. *every house looks_exactly the same*
3. *there's_a couple in the main room*

However, linking also occurs with other sounds. Mark where linking occurs in these excerpts from the interview, then check your answers with your teacher:

🎧 187

1. *I live in Maida Vale, which is not far from here at Regent's Park and the Academy...*
2. *It's basically a block of um, apartments – two or three-bedroom apartments – stacked on top of each other.*
3. *And they're often referred to as 'mansions'.*
4. *So your address is 96 Elgin Mansions...*
5. *And it's also close to an area called Little Venice*

138   *A Place I Know Well*

C Features of spoken English: elision and the glottal stop

(188)

When speaking quickly in English, people often miss out individual sounds at the ends of words – a process known as *elision*. For example, a speaker will say *las' night* instead of *last night*, *jus' got here* instead of *just got here*, or *trie' to* instead of *tried to*.

Another feature of natural spoken English is the *glottal stop*. The glottal stop occurs when the speaker constricts his or her throat and blocks the air stream completely. This results in the speaker not pronouncing fully the *-t* sound at the end of words such as *got* or *lot*, or the *-t-* sounds in words such as *bottle* or *kettle*.

This gap-fill exercise focuses on words which you probably know already, but whose pronunciation has changed because of elision or Scott's use of the glottal stop.

Try to fill in the gaps before you listen to the excerpts, and discuss your predictions with your teacher. Then listen and fill in the gaps.

1. I _____ there about a year... a _____ over a year ago.
2. it's actually a really nice _____ of London
3. And they're often _____ to as 'mansions'.
4. so I _____ know exactly what the definition of a mansionette is
5. _____ people renting in London – certainly people of my age – if they're renting _____ to be sharing with someone
6. _____ because the, the, the rent in London is quite expensive
7. we _____ on well
8. I was looking for something a _____ cheaper even then
9. which was _____ fun
10. so I think what I've _____ now is luxury _____ to that
11. by sharing a house with a few others we can _____ to rent there
12. it's also close to an area _____ Little Venice
13. so I _____ to make the most of the river by taking up rowing and going for runs along the river
14. Regent's Park and Lords are the _____ of highlights of that area.
15. I'll probably _____ back into running er, when the weather picks up a _____

UNIT 11: Scott

5. Further Language Development

A Extension exercise

Fill in the blanks in these new sentences with words you heard during Scott's interview. The words are listed in the box to help you.

> crammed   distance   door   for   get   keen
> most   part   rent   share   single   term

1. I specifically asked for a _____ room, not a double.
2. I know you're not very happy being away from your family, but you've got to try to make the _____ of your time here.
3. Do you _____ on well with your mother? I always argue with mine.
4. I won't have any cake, thanks. I'm not very _____ on sweet things.
5. It was a wonderful flat, but the _____ was too much for me on my own, so now I'm trying to find somewhere cheaper.
6. Do you know the meaning of the Latin _____ *tempus fugit*?
7. It's a beautiful day. Would you like to go _____ a walk?
8. You can _____ my umbrella if you like. It's big enough for two.
9. In which _____ of Paris do you live? Perhaps I know it.
10. When we go away we always get the people next _____ to feed our cat.
11. At my last job there were nearly 20 of us _____ into one small office the size of my living room.
12. Our flat is walking _____ from the tube, so we hardly use the car during the week.

B Phrasal verbs

Scott uses a number of phrasal verbs in his interview. A *phrasal verb* is a verb followed by a preposition or adverb or both which changes the meaning of the main verb, as in this example:

'When are you going to give up smoking?'

Insert the missing preposition in each sentence. The phrasal verbs are taken from Scott's interview:

1. My parents took _____ golf when they retired.
2. Do you get _____ well with your brother?
3. I didn't open a book all summer, so it's going to be hard to get back _____ studying again.

140   *A Place I Know Well*

4. As soon as the weather picks _____ I'm going to start cycling to work.
5. At last! I've been looking _____ that sock for ages.

C Colloquial English

Scott uses lots of colloquial English words and phrases in his interview. Colloquial English is found in informal spoken and written English, for example, when friends chat or write emails.

Try to fit the words in the box into the sentences below. Two of the words are used twice:

> afford   age   at   bit   fun   lucky
> most   much   same   stage   while

1. I can't really _____ that much. Have you got anything a _____ cheaper?
2. We're very _____ because our flat is walking distance from where we work.
3. You look exactly the _____ as when we were students! You haven't changed a bit.
4. I left home a _____ over a year ago, but I still miss my family.
5. I don't really like living out in the suburbs, but it's all I can _____, so I'm trying to make the _____ of it.
6. The party was great _____, but I had to leave early to get the last bus home.
7. The snow looked beautiful at first, but it got a bit _____ after a _____.
8. I'm at bit busy _____ the moment. Can I call you back?
9. I don't see the problem! Most people my _____ stay out late on Friday nights. Why should I be any different?
10. At one _____ I was thinking of giving up university and getting a job, but I'm glad I didn't.

6. Transcript 🎧 189   I: Interviewer   S: Scott

I: Can you tell me where you live in London?
S: OK, yes. Er, at the moment I live in **(1) Maida Vale**, which is not far from here at **(2) Regent's Park** and **(3) the Academy**. Um, I moved there about a year... **(4) a bit over a year ago**. So it's a... it's actually a really nice part of London. Very quiet, very... um, wide streets. Everyone lives in **(5) mansionettes**, so you walk down the street and every house looks exactly the same – or every block of apartments looks exactly the same.
I: Did you say 'mansionettes' or?
S: Yeah, mansionettes. Um...
I: What do you mean by...?
S: Er, that's **(6) the term**... It's certainly a term I wasn't familiar with until I came to London. Er... I think it's... I think the French um, are particularly **(7) keen on** mansionettes. It's **(8) basically** a block of um, apartments, two or three-bedroom apartments, **(9) stacked on top of each other**.
I: Mhm, mm.
S: And they're often referred to as 'mansions'. So my address is 96 Elgin Mansions, which is a block of apartments. And then next door is another block called Biddulph Mansions, but they're all er... So your address is 96 Elgin Mansions, Elgin Avenue, London.
I: I see.
S: Um, so I don't know exactly what the definition of a mansionette is, but um, I use it refer to the **(10) red-brick**-type **housing** that we have in Maida Vale which is um, three or four... Maida Vale is full of three or four-bed... three or two-bedroom apartments, basically and I, I live in a three-bedroom one with um, three other people, so there's **(11) a couple** in the main room and then there's me and another um, single **(12) guy** in the other single room.
I: So do you share a living room and a kitchen?
S: We, we share the living room and we share kitchen and we share bathroom. Um, most people **(13) renting** in London – certainly people of my age, if they're renting – **(14) tend to be sharing with someone** er, just because the, the, the rent in London is quite expensive um, so... I'm quite lucky – I've got a lovely place and um, I'm only sharing with three other people and we, we get on well and we live like a family, really. We share the cooking. But er, when I first got to London **(15) obviously** I was looking for something a bit cheaper even then and I was sharing with... up to ten people **(16) at one stage** – ten **(17) Aussies**, **(18) Kiwis**, Germans **(19) all crammed into one place** in **(20) Shepherd's Bush**. So that was my first experience of... which was **(21) great fun**, but er, **(22) it gets a bit much after a while**. It's pretty much like living in a, in **(23) a hostel**.
I: Yes.
S: Er, so I think what I've got now is luxury compared to that and I'm very happy with Maida Vale and it's close to everything so um... Yeah, I'm not planning to move any time soon.
I: It's quite a rich area, I think.
S: Yeah, yeah. **(24) I certainly couldn't afford to buy a house there**. Um, but by sharing a house with a few others we can afford to rent there. So yeah, it is quite a, quite an **(25) affluent area**. Er, it's not far from **(26) St John's Wood** which is... there's particularly a lot of rich, rich houses there.
I: Mhm, mm.
S: Um, and it's walking distance to Lord's cricket ground which, for me as a cricket fan, is a good thing. And it's also close to an area called Little Venice which is... er, which I never knew existed in London, but there's a lot of **(27) canals** around London with um, with, like, canal boats like um, **(28) gondolas**, basically, er, similar to Venice, so they call it Little Venice and er, that's a nice place to visit, too.
I: So have you walked round at all?
S: Yeah, yeah, I walk along the canals um, in summer. You can walk all the way along the canals to Regent's Park, **(29) Camden Town**. So it's all about making the most of the area that you're living in at the time, so **(30) prior to this** I was in, in **(31) Hammersmith** which is on **(32) the Thames**, so I tried to make the most of the river by **(33) taking up (34) rowing** and going for runs along the river. So now, um, Maida Vale, it's the canals and Regent's Park and Lords are the sort of highlights of that area.
I: Do you think you're slowing down as you're getting older, 'cos er...?
S: Not planning to!
I: Well, first you were **(35) jogging** and things along the river. Now you're walking along the canal bank...
S: I see what you mean, yes!
I: ... and watching cricket.
S: Er, um, yeah, I've, I'm certainly doing less exercise than I was two years ago, but um... yeah, that's just **(36) a cyclical thing** with me and **(37) I'll probably get back into running** er, **(38) when the weather picks up a bit** – might start doing a bit more of that.

A Place I Know Well

7. Words and Phrases

1. Maida Vale – an area of north London which lies between Paddington, St John's Wood and Kilburn
2. Regent's Park – the area around the Royal Park in the northern part of central London
3. the Academy – the interview took place at the Royal Academy of Music in London
4. a bit over – slightly over (in this case maybe a year and one or two months)
5. mansionettes – houses which look like mansions from the outside, but which contain separate flats/apartments
6. the term – the expression
7. keen on – like something
8. basically – an adverb used when giving a simple explanation of something
9. stacked on top of each other – one flat is on top of the other
10. red-brick – bricks are hard blocks of baked clay used to build houses, walls, etc.
11. a couple – two people who are considered together, usually in a romantic relationship
12. guy – an informal word for a man
13. renting – paying money to live somewhere
14. tend to be sharing with someone – are often/usually sharing with someone
15. obviously – clearly, evidently
16. at one stage – at one time in his life
17. Aussies – an informal word for people from Australia
18. Kiwis – an informal word for people from New Zealand (because a bird called the kiwi is the native bird of New Zealand)
19. all crammed into one place – the flat was full of people
20. Shepherd's Bush – a district of west London which borders Hammersmith
21. great fun – a good laugh; I enjoyed myself
22. it gets a bit much after a while – it becomes a bit difficult over time
23. a hostel – a very cheap type of hotel where each room contains two or more beds
24. certainly couldn't afford to buy a house there – he doesn't have enough money to buy a house there
25. affluent – desribing an area where people have a lot of money
26. St John's Wood – a district of northwest London near Regent's Park
27. canals – waterways which have been created by digging passages out of the ground
28. gondolas – narrow boats with flat bottoms found in Venice, which Scott thinks are similar to the narrow boats found on London's canals
29. Camden Town – an area of northwest London close to Regent's Park
30. prior to this – (formal) before this
31. Hammersmith – an area in west London on the north bank of the River Thames
32. the Thames – the river which flows through London (pronounced 'Temse')
33. taking up – starting an activity
34. rowing – sitting in a boat and pulling on oars to move it through the water
35. jogging – running slowly and steadily in order to exercise
36. a cyclical thing – something which happens in cycles, i.e. something he does every few years
37. I'll probably get back into running – I'll probably start running regularly again
38. when the weather picks up a bit – when the weather improves (The interview took place in winter.)

UNIT 12 Ingse

1. Pre-Listening Comprehension

A Schema building

Ingse is a woman from Bergen, a city on the west coast of Norway. How much do you know about Norway? Answer true or false.

1. _____ Norway became independent from Denmark in 1905.
2. _____ The coastline of Norway contains many *fjords*—deep inlets along the coastline—and thousands of islands.
3. _____ In northern Norway the sun does not set from the middle of May until late July.
4. _____ Norway exports more oil than Russia and Saudi Arabia.

144   *A Place I Know Well*

B Discussion

Discuss the questions in small groups. Share your answers with the class.

1. Do you know anything else about Norway?
2. Do you know what a Norwegian accent sounds like?
3. Have you ever visited Norway? Would you like to? Why or why not?

C Normalisation

190

This exercise is designed to help you get used to Ingse's voice. Try to guess the missing words before you listen and discuss these with your teacher. Then listen and fill in the gaps.

1. Bergen is the _____ biggest city in Norway.
2. Bergen is _____ by seven _____.
3. In _____ a _____ destroyed a lot of buildings in the old town.
4. Bergen used to be famous for its _____ industry.

D Anticipating the next word

191 to 196
197 to 202

Listen to tracks 191–196. There is a word missing from the end of each excerpt. Try to guess the missing word and write it down. Then listen to tracks 197–202 to check your answers. How well did you guess?

1. _____
2. _____
3. _____
4. _____
5. _____
6. _____

Bergen

UNIT 12: *Ingse*

2. Listening Comprehension

A Questions

Ingse talks in general about Bergen. Listen and answer the questions.

1. Which is the most common fish reared in the fish farms off the coast of Bergen?
2. What is the opposite of the adjective 'farmed'?
3. What is one of the seven mountains surrounding Bergen?
4. Which countries can you take a ferry to from Bergen?
5. Which two types of boats does Ingse mention?

B True/False

Ingse talks about where she lives in Bergen. Answer true or false. Be prepared to give reasons for your answers.

1. _____ Ingse doesn't live in central Bergen.
2. _____ Ingse used to have to climb up a hill every day when she came back from school.
3. _____ Ingse lives on the ground floor of her block of flats.
4. _____ Ingse prefers the view from her flat in the winter, when the trees are bare.
5. _____ Bergen is covered with snow during the winter months.
6. _____ Bergen is famous for its bad weather.

C Gap-fill

Ingse talks about skiing and fjords. Before you listen, try to predict which words, or which **types** of words (nouns, adjectives, prepositions, parts of verbs, etc.) will fit in the gaps. Then listen and check your answers.

1. It takes Ingse _____ _____ to _____ to the nearest ski resort.
2. At the ski resort you can do _____ or _____ skiing.
3. Ingse says it is not _____ to go skiing in Norway.
4. Ingse says cross-country skiing is like _____, but with skis on your feet.
5. The interviewer asks if it's _____ enough to go to the _____ in the summer in Norway.
6. Ingse says a fjord looks like a _____, but the water is _____.
7. This is because a fjord occurs when the _____ makes its way into the _____.

A Place I Know Well

8. Cruise liners from England and the _____ often enter the fjords because the water is very _____.

9. In summer the mountains near Bergen don't have any _____.

10. Bergen is _____ in having a glacier so close to the _____.

11. In _____ and _____ it's possible to go _____ on the glacier in the morning and then _____ in the fjord in the _____.

D True/False

Ingse talks about the cost of living in Norway. Answer true or false. Be prepared to give reasons for your answers.

1. _____ Ingse spends a couple of days in England every month.
2. _____ Ingse says food is what tourists find most expensive in Bergen.
3. _____ In Norway 0.4 of a litre of beer costs around £5.
4. _____ A large pizza in a restaurant costs around £25.
5. _____ Cosmetics in England now cost nearly as much as those in Norway.
6. _____ It's usual for Norwegians to meet their friends in each other's houses rather than in restaurants or pubs.
7. _____ Bergen city centre is very quiet in the evenings.

3. Interesting Language Points

A The present perfect simple

We use the present perfect simple to talk about things we have done in a period of time leading up to the present. This is why the interviewer says:

> *I've never been* to Bergen.

Later in the interview, when talking about the price of takeaway pizzas, Ingse says:

> It's a long time since *I've done* that, because of the prices.

B *would* for past habit

We often use *would* + verb to talk about past habit, as well as *used to* + verb. In spoken English the word *would* is generally replaced by *'d*.

When talking about Ingse's childhood the interviewer says:

> But *you'd walk* down in the mornings?

She could equally have said:

> But you *used to walk* down in the mornings?

Here are some more examples of this usage:

> 'When we were kids, *we'd* often *camp* out in the garden in the summer.'
> 'In my last job *we'd finish* work at 5 on Fridays.'
> 'When my grandparents were living here *they'd have* a wood fire in the winter.'

C Features of informal spoken English

Colloquial language
Ingse uses several colloquial expressions which are common in informal spoken and written English, such as two friends chatting, emails between friends, and so on, but not in more formal English such as lectures, speeches and letters to companies.

For example, Ingse says:

> *yeah* instead of *yes* **and** *quid* instead of *pounds*

Imprecision

Informal spoken English is less precise than formal English and we often use words such as *stuff* or *things* instead of being more precise in what we are referring to. Look at this excerpt from the interview:

Interviewer: <u>Things</u> like cosmetics – are they expensive?

Ingse: It is expensive, but I think er, a few years back we could go to England or other places and buy really cheap <u>stuff</u>.

Later you hear:

Ingse: You have to do the climbing then ... with rods and <u>stuff</u>.

Exaggeration

This occurs a great deal in informal spoken English. Look at these very common informal examples and their more formal equivalents:

Informal: I've been waiting <u>for ages</u>!
Formal: I've been waiting since 6.30.

Informal: It cost <u>a fortune</u>!
Formal: It was quite expensive, actually.

Informal: I'm <u>baking</u>!
Formal: I am feeling a bit warm.

Informal: I'm <u>starving</u>!
Formal: I am quite hungry.

Informal: I'm <u>dying of thirst</u>!
Formal: I am quite thirsty.

During the interview Ingse says *we have loads of snow*. In a more formal situation she would be more likely to say *we get a great deal of snow*.

Later in the interview she talks about Bergen at night and uses the word *dead* to mean *quiet* in the following excerpt:

It's lively in town. I don't mean it's <u>dead</u> because it's expensive.

D Features of a Norwegian accent

(207)

1. In general Norwegians tend to pronounce the 'th' sound in words such as *the* and *these* as 'd'. Listen to these extracts:

   yeah, the fish industry and trading with Europe
   we're part of the seven mountains
   I can see the fjord...
   That's not expensive in Norway any more.

2. Many Norwegians tend to over-emphasise the letter combination 'oo', as found in the words *too* or *school*. Listen:

(208)

   not too old
   to get home from school

3. The word *fjord* in Norwegian is written *fjørd*, with the line through the letter 'o' meaning that the ø is pronounced 'oe'. Listen to how Ingse tends to pronounce the letter 'o' in English as 'oe':

(209)

   They're starting off with cod now, but it's mostly salmon.
   Not to go, no.
   Which is unique that we have a glacier so close to the coast.
   we tend to spend more time at home

E Standard intonation patterns

There is a strong tendency for a speaker's voice to rise or fall during certain speech acts, although there are often exceptions, as we have seen with Scott's voice tending to rise at the end of statements (Unit 1). There are, however, examples of five standard intonation patterns in the interview with Ingse. Read and listen to the examples.

(210)

Fall on statements

Ingse's voice falls at the end of these statements:

It's a small city...
in 1916 we had a big fire
They're starting off with cod now...
And actually one of the mountains is an island.
So it's quite crowded.

150   *A Place I Know Well*

Rise for yes/no questions

The interviewer's voice rises when she asks questions to which the answer can be '*yes*' or '*no*':

> Now you come from Norway?
> Is the centre of town very modern?
> Was it a big fishing industry in Bergen?

Falling intonation with question tags when the speaker is expecting confirmation of what they've just said:

> I think Bergen's the second biggest city in Norway, isn't it?

Falling intonation when giving yes/no answers, or answers which convey agreement:

> **Interviewer:** I think Bergen's the second biggest city in Norway, isn't it?
>
> **Ingse:** It is.
>
> **Interviewer:** Was it a big fishing industry in Bergen? Lots of ships?
>
> **Ingse:** Yes. Lots of ships . . .

Falling intonation for **Wh questions**

The term *Wh questions* refers to questions which begin with these words: *What . . . ? When . . . ? Which . . . ? Why . . . ?* and, confusingly, *How . . . ?* Listen to the interviewer's intonation with these Wh questions:

> So <u>how</u> many floors?
> <u>Which</u> floor do you live on?
> In the winter, if you want to go skiing outside Bergen, <u>where</u> do you go?
> <u>What</u> about the sea?

UNIT 12: *Ingse* 151

4. Further Listening Practice

A Recognising individual words in a stream of speech (Dictation)

🎧 215 to 🎧 221

Work with a partner. Listen to the excerpts from Ingse's interview and write them down. Then check with another pair.

1. _____
2. _____
3. _____
4. _____
5. _____
6. _____
7. _____

B Intonation practice

🎧 222

In Section E of the previous section – Interesting Language Points – we looked at some standard intonation patterns including the following:

- Falling intonation at the end of statements
- Rising intonation when the speaker is expecting a yes/no answer
- Falling intonation when asking 'Wh' questions.

Read the following excerpts from the interview and decide whether the speaker's voice will rise or fall (⟋ ⟍) on the highlighted words, then listen and check your answers.

1. And er, nowadays we also get the small cabin cruisers.
2. We don't get as much snow as up in the mountains.
3. Do they still do fishing now in Bergen?
4. It's a rainy city.
5. You can go where you like.
6. Are there any islands out at sea?
7. Do you have good views?
8. Can you go skiing in Bergen?
9. How much is a pound, now?
10. What about er, something like a pizza?

C Contractions

🎧 223

Contractions are common in informal spoken and written English, such as two friends chatting, emails between friends, and so on, but not in more formal English such as lectures, speeches and letters to companies. With a partner, practise saying the contracted forms of these phrases.

> do not   have not   is not   it is   they are   we are

Now look at the following excerpts from the interview and put in the appropriate contractions. Then listen to find out if you were correct.

1. They are starting off with cod now, but it is mostly salmon, yes.
2. We do not get as much snow as up in the mountains
3. But it is salty water.
4. Because they are very, very deep.
5. I have not been here for a while, now.
6. And a pint, which is not a pint any more . . .
7. It is a long time since I have done that . . .
8. And then one evening, we are at my house . . .

Bodo, Norway

UNIT 12: *Ingse*

5. Further Language Development

A Extension exercise   Fill in the blanks in these new sentences with words you heard during Ingse's interview. The words are listed in the box to help you.

> afford   common   compared   deep   enough
> expensive   flats   floor   harbour   loads
> rather   still   surrounded   tastes   view

1. Bonn is quite a small city _____ to Hamburg.
2. I find Mumbai very stressful because you're _____ by people all the time.
3. Do you _____ go rock climbing these days, or have you stopped?
4. We don't eat much beef because it's so _____, but sometimes we'll get a small fillet steak for a treat.
5. The blue tit is now the most _____ bird in England. You can see them in nearly every garden.
6. I think Swiss chocolate _____ much better than American chocolate.
7. Yesterday we went for a walk down to the _____ and booked a fishing trip for this coming Sunday.
8. We used to live on the 10th _____ of a block of _____ in Camden Town, but then we bought this house when we decided to start a family.
9. The _____ from this window is wonderful in autumn when all the leaves on the trees in that wood over there change colour.
10. You can tell Valentina's got _____ of money. She always goes on expensive holidays and you never see her in the same outfit twice.
11. Do you think it will be warm _____ just to wear a T-shirt, or should I wear a jumper over it?
12. Before you dive into a swimming pool, it's a good idea to check first how _____ the water is.
13. On Friday evenings we prefer to stay in _____ than going out because everywhere's so crowded.
14. I'd love to come to Italy, but I really can't _____ it at the moment. I've just heard I've got to pay out nearly £5,000 to get the roof repaired.

A Place I Know Well

B Prepositions

Fill in the missing prepositions in the gaps below. The sentences are all based on the language used in Ingse's interview.

1. She's got a beautiful house in the country surrounded _____ fields.
2. London is very expensive compared _____ Berlin.
3. _____ the centre of the ring there was a tiny diamond.
4. We live _____ the ninth floor, which is fine so long as the elevator is working.
5. How much did you pay _____ your train ticket?
6. Please make yourself feel _____ home.
7. Shall we go out _____ dinner? I'm too tired to cook.
8. Sam lives _____ a block _____ flats overlooking a canal.
9. What _____ Sean? Would he like to come with us, do you think?
10. They put the wind farm miles out _____ sea, so it wouldn't spoil the view from the beach.

C Transformations

Change the word in each bracket which Ingse used in her interview to form a word which fits the gap:

1. I can smell (burnt) _____! Have you left something under the grill again?
2. Police are investigating the (disappear) _____ of two hitchhikers.
3. This used to be a really (industry) _____ area when I was growing up.
4. The one disadvantage of living in Bath is that it's very (hills) _____.
5. This soup is really (tastes) _____. How did you make it?
6. Her dissertation is on population (grew) _____ in southern Europe.
7. It seems that in Eastern Europe (farmed) _____ is becoming less and less popular with younger people.
8. It was only when the Queen (stand) _____ up that I realised she's even shorter than I am!
9. I can remember this (build) _____ going up!

UNIT 12: *Ingse*

6. Transcript 🎧 224   I: Interviewer   Ingse

I: OK. Now you come from Norway?
Ingse: Yes.
I: And you live in Bergen?
Ingse: Yes, I do.
I: I think Bergen's the second biggest city in Norway, isn't it?
Ingse: It is.
I: Yeah. I've never been to Bergen. Can you tell me what it's like, please?
Ingse: It's um . . . It's a small city and you've got... all the cities in Norway are small compared to England. But it's er, the city centre is small. It's situ . . . situated at a **(1) harbour** . . .
I: Mhm, hm.
Ingse: . . . and er, surrounded by seven mountains.
I: Oh, that sounds nice.
Ingse: Yes. And **(2) basically** I think that's, you know, gives you an idea what it looks like.
I: Hmm. Is the centre of the town very modern?
Ingse: Yes, er, not too old because in, in 1916 we had a big fire so all the old houses, they burnt, so they had to build new, new houses, new buildings, so **(3) comparatively**, yes. But we have old parts of Bergen along the, the harbour – **(4) the quayside**.
I: Mhm, hm. So um . . . Was it a big **(5) fishing industry** in Bergen? Lots of ships?
Ingse: Yes. Lots of ships, and not only... yeah, the fish industry and trading with Europe.
I: Um, do they still do fishing now in Bergen?
Ingse: No.
I: No. So it's finished.
Ingse: No. You have the **(6) fisheries** and they come in with er, with er, er . . . from the, from the fish farms.
I: Oh, right.
Ingse: Yes, they, they have places in, not . . . along the quayside where they actually come in with fish from the . . . er . . .
I: From these farms.
Ingse: Farms.
I: Right. What, what kind of fish are they?
Ingse: **(7) Salmon**.
I: Mhm, hm.
Ingse: They're starting off with **(8) cod** now, but it's mostly salmon, yes.
I: OK. Now for us in England, salmon is the most expensive fish. Is that the same in Norway?
Ingse: Not any more. When I was a little girl it was, was a special thing if we had salmon, but nowadays it's, **(9) it's common**. It's the cheapest one you can get, more or less, yes.

I: Is that because it is farmed?
Ingse: Yes, it is farmed. It's . . . If you buy the wild one, which some people think it tastes better – I think it do, yeah.
I: You think it does?
Ingse: Does, yes. And er, then you pay more.
I: I see.
Ingse: Yeah.
I: So you said there's seven mountains around Bergen. Are there any islands out at sea?
Ingse: Oh yes, it's er . . . It's not right out to, to the ocean. We have got a coastline with many islands.
I: Mhm, hm.
Ingse: And actually one of the mountains is an island.
I: Really?
Ingse: (laughs) Yes.
I: That must be nice.
Ingse: So it's a, **(10) it's a bit cheating saying** we're part of the seven mountains, but it's, it's like when you are in Bergen it looks like just er, a **(11) fjord**?
I: Mhm, hm.
Ingse: Yeah, because you don't see the ocean from, from the, from the city.
I: Um, do you have **(12) ferries** going from Bergen to . . . I don't know – Finland or England or?
Ingse: To er, England, yes. Denmark . . .
I: Mhm, hm.
Ingse: Er, Iceland.
I: Really?
Ingse: Smyril Line to Iceland. Faroe Island.
I: Faroe? Faroes.
Ingse: Faroes, yes.
I: Oh, gosh! So there's a lot of visitors, I suppose, come, come to Bergen? It must be full of people . . .
Ingse: Oh, yes. Oh, yes. And cruisers, cruise liners? And during the summer there can be seven or ten.
I: At the harbour?
Ingse: Yeah, in, in one day.
I: Gosh.
Ingse: So it's quite crowded. And er, nowadays we also get the small **(13) cabin cruisers**.
I: Mhm, hm.
Ingse: Quite a few of them, with people being rich in Norway now they can afford cabin cruisers, and they come, rather than just going out to the islands, they come into town, yeah.
I: Um, do you live in the centre of the town?

156   *A Place I Know Well*

Ingse: No, I live outside.
I: OK. Can you tell me about where you live?
Ingse: Yeah (laughs).
I: Is that on a mountain or . . .
Ingse: No, it's flat, which I think is nice, because where I grew up was on a hillside and every day er, coming home I had to climb the hills. I actually er, from school when I was a child, I went, I went on **(14) a funicular** to . . .
I: Is that, is that a kind of train?
Ingse: Yes, it's like a cable car thing.
I: OK. Right.
Ingse: Yeah, a train, yes, taking you up to the mountains.
I: Mhm, hm.
Ingse: So on the way, to get home from school I can go on that one.
I: OK.
Ingse: Yeah (laughs).
I: But you'd walk down in the mornings?
Ingse: I would walk down in the morning, yes. And I . . . I could go up on that one in the evening, afternoon.
I: Right. So where you live it's flat. Do you live in a house, or?
Ingse: No, in a um, in a blocks [sic – block] of flats.
I: OK. So how many floors?
Ingse: Three floors, yes.
I: Which floor do you live on?
Ingse: On the third . . . er, se . . . In English it's the second!
I: Second.
Ingse: Yes.
I: OK. So that's the very top?
Ingse: Yeah.
I: Do you, do you have good views from there?
Ingse: A marvellous view, yeah, especially in the winter when the leaves, leaves are off the trees.
I: Why is that nice? Why?
Ingse: Because then I can see further – I can see the fjord and I can see the mountains. And the mountains are white with snow.
I: Oh, right.
Ingse: But in the summer **(15) it's nice and cosy** with the trees, you know, the green trees.
I: OK. Um, you said about snow. Can you go skiing in Bergen?
Ingse: Yes, but we don't get as much snow as up in the mountains. **(16) We get spells of snow.** Like for a week.
I: Mhm, hm.
Ingse: And then **(17) we have loads of snow.**
I: Right.
Ingse: I mean really much. And we can go skiing where we live. But then it disappears again and starts raining. It's a rainy city.
I: Is it?

Ingse: Famous for its raining, yeah. (laughs)
I: So in the winter, if you want to go skiing outside Bergen, where do you go?
Ingse: I would go, I would drive sort of 45 minutes and that would take me to a ski resort where I can do downhill or cross-country skiing. There are tracks.
I: Mhm, hm.
Ingse: Yeah.
I: OK. Is it very expensive to go skiing?
Ingse: No. It's just the petrol to get there.
I: Oh, you don't have to pay . . .
Ingse: Not, not to go, no. The . . . **(18) It's open landscape.** You can go where you like.
I: Oh, so it's not like in Switzerland where you're going up in a cable car and then skiing down a mountain. This is . . .
Ingse: If you do downhill it's – that's the nicest way – or easiest way – to do it. But if you do cross-country, you do like walking, only you have your skis on.
I: Oh, OK.
Ingse: It's not like in, in, er . . . When you see the competitions?
I: Yeah.
Ingse: They have these fantastic **(19) tracks.**
I: Yeah.
Ingse: But you can also go skiing wherever you like in the mountains.
I: I see.
Ingse: So you just know where to go and where to, to go down again.
I: OK. Um, what about the sea? Do you, do you go to the seaside at all in the summer? Is it warm enough to go to the seaside?
Ingse: Yeah, but the seaside is not the seaside the way you think of the seaside here. We don't get the **(20) long stretches of beaches.** We have small beaches and we, we can certainly go swimming. It's nice and warm in, in, in the fjords, for example.
I: Just explain what a fjord is. Is it like a lake, or?
Ingse: Yeah, but it's er, it's, it looks like, when you are along a fjord, it looks like a lake. But it's salty water. It's actually the, the ocean making its way into the, into the countryside.
I: OK. So, so . . . yeah, so the water's salty. In theory, then, you could, you could swim out to sea from a fjord?
Ingse: Oh, yes. And, and the boats are coming in, the cruise liners are coming in from, from England, from [sic – the] Mediterranean. And they can come in, in, in the fjords.
I: OK. Do you get . . .
Ingse: Because they're very, very deep.
I: I see.
Ingse: Yes.
I: But then it must be really cold to go swimming in a fjord.

Ingse: No, even if you have the, the water from the glacier, it isn't. It's ... because **(21) it's sheltered** ...
I: OK.
Ingse: It's getting nice and warm. But it's not as salt ... the water is not as salty as out in the ocean, because it mingles with, well it's mixed with the water from rains and **(22) the glacier**.
I: OK. Um, in summer do the mountains near Bergen, do they still have snow on them?
Ingse: No. Only the glacier.
I: OK.
Ingse: Which is unique that we have a glacier so close to the coast.
I: Mhm.
Ingse: You can actually stand... If you go up on the glacier in the summer ...
I: Mhm.
Ingse: ... you can see the, the ocean from there.
I: That must be beautiful.
Ingse: Yeah, it is, yeah. And you can go swimming er ... Well, in the morning you can drive up to the glacier and do some skiing, and then you come down in the evening and go swimming in the fjord.
I: What time of year would that be?
Ingse: In July – June, July. In August the snow on the, on er, on the glacier disappears and you have to know your way. You have to do the climbing then.
I: Right.
Ingse: With **(23) rods and stuff like that**.
I: OK. Mhm. It just sounds absolutely wonderful. I must go there one day.
Ingse: You should do. It's expensive, though.
I: How? How does it compare with prices in England, then?
Ingse: Er, I haven't been here for a while now, but the beer is what is er, the worst thing for tourists, of course, because when being on holiday you want to have a, a drink at night.
I: Yeah.
Ingse: And **(24) a pint**, which isn't a pint any more – you just get 0.4 litre ...
I: OK.
Ingse: ... and it can cost you about – how much is a pound, now? It can cost you about 60, 65 kronor, which is er, **(25) five quid**?
I: Yeah. Really? Five pounds?
Ingse: Yeah.
I: For just for one drink?
Ingse: Yeah, which is 0.4. It isn't even a pint! (laughs)
I: OK. What about er, something like a pizza? If you order **(26) a takeaway pizza**, um, say to feed two people, how much do you pay for that?

Ingse: I think... It's a long time since I've done that, because of the prices, but I think it's about 200 and 250 kronor... 280, perhaps, which again is £25.
I: Just for a pizza.
Ingse: Yeah. How much would that be in England? But that's a huge one – that's a big one.
I: OK. Well, our biggest one would be maybe £15.
Ingse: Yeah.
I: But not, not more than that. Oh dear. Hmm. What about um, clothes? Are they expensive?
Ingse: No, they're not. That's not expensive in Norway any more. Compared ... no, compared to the other prices.
I: Things like **(27) cosmetics** – are they expensive?
Ingse: It is expensive, but I think er, a few years back we could go to England or other places and buy really **(28) cheap stuff**. But I think **(29) the prices are levelling out**.
I: OK. Um, if it costs so much money to go for a beer or, or go for dinner, then it, it must stop you going out?
Ingse: It does. What we do, we meet at each other [sic – other's] places rather than going out.
I: Mhm, hm.
Ingse: Er, we tend to spend more time at home or inviting friends for a meal or for a drink.
I: Mhm.
Ingse: And then one evening we're at my house and then another day or evening we go and see somebody else.
I: OK. So you still have a social life?
Ingse: Oh, yeah.
I: But it's in houses rather than pubs or restaurants?
Ingse: Yeah, yeah.
I: Mhm. OK. Mhm.
Ingse: The students do go out, of course. It's lively in town. I don't mean it's dead because it's expensive. Because it's [sic there's] quite a lot going on at weekends. Thursday, Friday, Saturday – maybe Wednesday as well – so ... And the students are going out for, for drinks. And people do go out for meals, as course, but not as much as in England.
I: Right. OK. So more for special occasions.
Ingse: Yeah. For me, that would be.
I: OK. How can the students afford it? Do they pay cheaper prices for beer?
Ingse: (laughs) No, they just spend it! (laughs)

7. Words and Phrases

1. **a harbour** – an area of calm water usually sheltered by a wall near the land where ships are safe
2. **basically** – an adverb used when the speaker is giving a simple explanation or description of something
3. **comparatively** – an adverb used when considering two things, e.g. 'The air in central London is very polluted, but it's comparatively fresh out here in the suburbs.'
4. **the quayside** – the area where boats can be tied up and loaded or unloaded
5. **fishing industry** – the commercial process of obtaining and preparing fish for consumption
6. **fisheries** – another way of saying fish farms
7. **salmon** – a large fish with pink flesh which lives in the sea, but swims up rivers to lay its eggs
8. **cod** – a large sea fish with white flesh which lives in the North Atlantic
9. **it's common** – it's quite usual
10. **it's a bit cheating** – [sic – it's cheating a bit] it's not quite telling the truth; it's a little bit dishonest
11. **a fjord** – a long strip of sea between steep hills – found especially along the coasts of Norway and New Zealand's South Island
12. **ferries** – boats which provide a regular service transporting passengers and vehicles across an area of water
13. **cabin cruisers** – boats powered by motors with one or more rooms for sleeping in
14. **a funicular** – a railway which travels up and down a steep slope and is pulled by a cable
15. **it's nice and cosy** – the normal meaning is comfortable and pleasant, as in this example: 'This room is nice and cosy in winter when we light the fire.'
16. **We get spells of snow.** – We get short periods of snow lasting a few days or a week.
17. **we have loads of snow** – we have a lot of snow
18. **It's open landscape.** – A very common expression in both Sweden and Norway, where the people are very proud of the fact that landowners are not allowed to prevent people accessing their land for relaxation – walking, skiing, picnics, etc.
19. **tracks** – paths in the snow made especially for cross-country skiers to follow
20. **long stretches of beaches** – long, narrow areas of beaches all along the coast, as Ingse observed in England
21. **it's sheltered** – it's protected from the wind
22. **the glacier** – a large mass of ice which moves extremely slowly
23. **rods and stuff like that** – Here Ingse is referring to the special equipment used when climbing on glaciers. Rods are poles made of wood or metal.
24. **a pint** – a measure for liquid used in the UK – one pint = just under half a litre
25. **five quid** – (slang) five pounds; £5
26. **a takeaway pizza** – a pizza which you buy from a shop or restaurant, or have delivered, normally to eat at home
27. **cosmetics** – make-up, creams and powders used to improve your appearance and the condition of your skin
28. **cheap stuff** – (informal) inexpensive things
29. **the prices are levelling out** – the prices are becoming similar because British and European prices are rising and catching up with Norwegian prices

UNIT 13 Anne

1. Pre-Listening Comprehension

A Schema building

We heard Anne talking about a typical day in Unit 9. Just over a year ago Anne and her husband decided to relocate to the Greek island of Crete, near the resort of Sissi. How much do you know about Greece and Crete? Circle the correct answer.

1. Greece is known as the birthplace of democracy, Western philosophy and drama, and **Renaissance painting / the Olympic Games / the first Pyramids**.

2. Greece has **14 / 140 / 1400** islands, the largest of which is Crete.

3. Crete was the centre of the **Minoan / Babylonian / Assyrian** civilisation, the oldest civilisation in Europe.

4. The capital of Crete is **Argostoli / Thessaloniki / Heraklion**.

B Discussion

Discuss the questions in small groups. Share your answers with the class.

1. Do you know anything else about Greece or Crete?
2. Why do you think Anne and her husband would make such a big life change as moving to Crete?
3. Do you know what an English Midlands accent sounds like?

C Normalisation

🎧 225

This exercise is designed to help you get used to Anne's voice. Before you listen, try to predict which words, or which **types** of words will fit in the gaps. Then listen and check your answers.

Interviewer: Um, you, you said when we met that um, you came to Sissi last 1) _____ and you fell in 2) _____ with it . . .

Anne: Mmm.

Interviewer: . . . and you decided to 3) _____, so how, how did that actually happen?

Anne: Um, it, it wasn't so much Sissi. I fell, I fell in love with 4) _____ a long time 5) _____ – my 6) _____ and I did. And we came on lots and lots of 7) _____ and we always said that we would 8) _____ to Greece, we always 9) _____ to do that.

Crete

UNIT 13: *Anne* 161

2. Listening Comprehension

A True/False
🎧 226

In this first exercise Anne talks about living and working on Crete. Listen and decide if each statement is True (T) or False (F). Give reasons for your answers.

1. _____ One of the reasons Anne fell in love with the resort of Sissi was the people.
2. _____ Anne lives in the centre of Sissi.
3. _____ Anne often has the afternoons free.
4. _____ Anne rarely has time to go to the beach.
5. _____ Anne's husband works mainly in a bar.
6. _____ Anne's company only pays her during the tourist season.
7. _____ Anne says a lot of British holiday reps who come to work in Greece stay there during the winter because it's so cheap.
8. _____ Anne says a lot of holiday reps work in ski resorts during the winter.

B Gap-fill
🎧 227

Anne talks about her life during the winter on Crete. Before you listen, try to predict which words, or which types of words will fit in the gaps. Then listen and check your answers.

1. The interviewer says it must be quite _____ for Anne to make the money from the _____ months she works last through the _____ months.
2. Anne says she and her husband live like the _____ during the winter.
3. They _____ olives with their friends in the winter.
4. The people in the *kafeneion** don't pay them, but they do _____ them.
5. When they're picking olives, Anne and her husband go to the kafeneion to eat every _____.
6. They eat with the _____.

---

* *kafeneion* – a typical coffee shop and social gathering place for people in towns and villages across Greece

162 *A Place I Know Well*

C Questions

(228)

Anne talks about eating out and what she did before moving to Crete. Listen and answer the questions.

1. What have gone up in Greece since they introduced the euro?
2. Where is it particularly expensive to eat in Sissi?
3. How much do Anne and her husband pay for a meal for two with drinks in the kafeneion?
4. What do the interviewer and her friend normally have to eat at lunchtime?
5. Where was Anne born?
6. How long did Anne and her husband live in Burton-on-Trent?
7. What runs through the centre of Burton-on-Trent?
8. Where did Anne work in Burton-on-Trent?

UNIT 13: *Anne* 163

3. Interesting Language Points

A The present simple

We generally use the present simple to talk about facts and things that we do regularly. Look at these examples from the interview:

> I _don't live_ in Sissi now, but I _live_ not too far away.
>
> I still _have_ time to socialise and enjoy the sun and the life . . .
>
> We _pick_ olives in the winter with our friends and they don't actually pay us, but they _own_ the kafeneion so they _feed_ us.

B The simple past with time expressions

We use the simple past to talk about completed actions in the past. We often use the simple past with a time expression. Look at these examples:

> You said _when_ we met that you came to Sissi _last year_ and you fell in love with it and you decided to stay. How did that actually happen?
>
> I fell in love with Greece _a long time ago._
>
> I started work this year _21st March_.
>
> _before_ we moved out here my husband and I lived in Burton-on-Trent _for nine years_

C The present perfect simple

We use the present perfect simple to talk about things which have happened during a period of time leading up to the present, as in these examples:

The interviewer asks:
   And _has_ it _worked out_?   (i.e. since you came to Sissi)

Later she says:
   We've noticed prices _have_ really _gone up_ in Greece over the last few years.

Anne agrees and says:
   They _have bumped up_ their prices a little bit.

D **have to** and **have got to**

We use these structures when the need to do something is external to the speaker. Remember *have got to* is more informal than *have to*. Look at this example from the interview:

Anne says:
> So <u>you've got to</u> make enough money, basically, in the summer to get you through the winter if you stay here.

E **used to do something**

We use *used to* to talk about past habits that are no longer habits now. Look at these examples:

> When I was a child I <u>used to go</u> swimming in this river.

> I <u>used to love</u> skiing, but then I broke my leg and I went off it.

> We <u>used to go</u> for a long walk every evening when we lived in the country.

In the interview Anne says:

> I <u>used to work</u> in the Bass Museum.

4. Further Listening Practice

A Recognising individual words in a stream of speech (Dictation)

🎧 229 to 🎧 238

Work with a partner. Listen to the excerpts from Anne's interview and write them down. Then check with another pair.

1. _____
2. _____
3. _____
4. _____
5. _____
6. _____
7. _____
8. _____
9. _____
10. _____

B Recognising sentence stress

🎧 239

Stressed words are the most important in spoken English because they carry the most meaning. Which words do you think Anne stresses in the following extracts?

1. we came on lots and lots of holidays
2. I've got no regrets.
3. I live in a traditional village up the road.
4. and he works in the tourist industry as well
5. I'll go right through to the end of October
6. We pick olives in the winter with our friends, and they don't actually pay us, but they own the kafeneion, so they feed us.
7. every night we're expected to go down to the kafeneion and we eat with the family
8. So our, our cost of living is minimal in the winter . . .

Now listen to find out if your predictions were correct.

166 *A Place I Know Well*

C Weak forms: *to, for* and *of*

(240)

The citation form of *to*, *for* and *of* often changes to a weaker form in spoken English which is not as clear. Before you listen to the following excerpts, try to fill in the missing words. Then listen to check your answers.

1. So you've got _____ make enough money, basically, in the summer _____, _____ get you through the winter . . .

2. a lot _____ the reps that um, that come out from the UK, they will go back

3. if they want _____ come back, which a lot _____ them do . . .

4. we're expected _____ go down _____ the kafeneion and we eat with the family

5. we don't have _____ make a massive amount

6. we can eat there, even when we pay, um, _____ sort of nine euros

7. Anne: . . . my husband and I lived in Burton-on-Trent . . .
   Interviewer: Oh. Right.
   Anne: . . . _____, _____ nine years

D Linking

(241) to (242)

Linking occurs when the end of one word *runs_into the start_of* the next word. It is very common in informal spoken English, but less so in more formal English, such as speeches or lectures.

The most common linking occurs between the letter *–s* at the end of a word when the next word begins with a vowel, as in this excerpt from the interview:

we came on lots_and lots_of holidays

However, linking also occurs with other sounds. Mark where linking occurs in these excerpts from the interview:

I live not too far away

I wanted to work here

but it's so lovely

and things like that

It sounds strange...

if you're on the coastline

E Some features of a Midlands accent

The glottal stop

The glottal stop occurs when the speaker constricts his or her throat and blocks the air stream completely. This results in the speaker not pronouncing fully the *−t* sound at the end of words such as *got* or *lot*, or the *−t−* sounds in words such as *bottle* or *kettle*. This is a common feature of many British accents, and is used particularly by younger people.

Underline where Anne uses a glottal stop in the following excerpts:

1. I don't live in Sissi now, but I live not too far away
2. Love it.
3. so I can get away from the holiday resort bit
4. It is just a, a short-term contract.
5. if they want to come back, which a lot of them do
6. we get food when we're out picking anyway
7. and we eat with the family

an' *instead of* **and**

It is a common feature of many British accents that speakers drop the letter *–d* at the end of the word *and*, as does Anne in this excerpt

> we came on lots an' lots of holidays an' we always said that we would retire to Greece . . .

Mark where Anne drops the letter *–d* in the following excerpts.

1. we came and holidayed on, in Sissi and just loved it . . .
2. We were going to try and do it now and not when we retired.
3. Um, and it's just such a lovely lifestyle.
4. I still have time to socialise and enjoy the sun and the life . . .
5. nine euros with drinks and food and meze

Pronunciation – **cup** /ʌ/ *and* **put** /ʊ/

Like many native speakers in northern England and the Midlands, Anne does not distinguish the vowel sound found in the word *cup* in standard English from the vowel sound found in *put*. Listen to how first Anne, and then your teacher, pronounce the following excerpts. Can you hear the differences?

> and <u>just loved</u> it
> I live in a traditional village <u>up</u> the road
> at <u>lunchtime</u>
> it's <u>just such</u> a lovely lifestyle
> enjoy the <u>sun</u>
> that <u>come</u> out from the UK
> we're very <u>much</u> village people
> they have <u>bumped</u> the prices up a little bit
> all my family live <u>up</u>, <u>up</u> north

5. Further Language Development

A Extension exercise Fill in the blanks in these new sentences with words you heard during Anne's interview. The words are listed in the box to help you.

> begged   brought   contract   hard   love
> off   on   massive   minimal   paid   pick
> retire   share   tourist   traditional

1. I fell in __ _____ with Christophe the first time I saw him.
2. I've got another 12 years until I _____. I could stop sooner, but then I'd get a smaller pension.
3. When I was a kid, I _____ my parents to let me have a kitten, but we couldn't 'cos my mum was allergic to cat fur.
4. You're getting very wet. Would you like to _____ my umbrella?
5. We get _____ really well with our neighbours. We always stop and have a chat when we see each other out in the garden or in the street.
6. Roast beef and Yorkshire pudding is a _____ Sunday lunch in Britain.
7. I run my own business so I can choose my own hours. I nearly always begin work at 8 and then knock _____ at around 4.
8. I think you're working too _____ – you look exhausted!
9. The _____ season in Greece lasts from May to October.
10. I got _____ £200 a week when I started work in 1995.
11. According to the _____ I only get four weeks' holiday a year, but they definitely said I'd get five weeks during the interview.
12. My best friend's sister is going to France this summer to pick grapes on a vineyard.
13. My Spanish is _____ so I'm going to have some lessons before we go back there on holiday.
14. Kim's parents live in a _____ house in the centre of Seoul. It's got five bedrooms and four bathrooms.
15. I was born in Athens, but my family moved to Kefalonia when I was a toddler and so I was _____ up there.

170   *A Place I Know Well*

B *get* and *got*

The verb *to get* occurs much more frequently in informal spoken English than in formal written English.

Look at the following sentences containing examples of phrases with the verb *to get* taken from Anne's interview. Insert *get* or *got* where appropriate.

1. I'm sorry, I can't come out tonight. I've still _____ lots of revision to do.
2. When I was younger I never used to _____ on with my parents, but I do now.
3. I _____ called in to see the manager yesterday.
4. I just don't know how I'm going to _____ through all this work.
5. It was tough changing careers in my 30s, but I've _____ no regrets.
6. Let's go out! I've just _____ paid for that project I did last month.
7. We try to _____ away to our country cottage every other weekend.
8. It was a really tough interview, but I _____ the job.

C Colloquial English

Anne, like Scott and Ingse, uses a lot of colloquial English words and phrases in her interview. Colloquial English is found in informal spoken and written English, for example when friends chat or write emails.

> bit   feel   geared up for   hard
> just up the road   to make it last   not too far from
> off the beaten track   worth it

Try to fit the words and phrases in the box into the sentences below.

1. Barnet is just another suburb of London now, but it's still got that village _____.
2. It was the most expensive holiday we've ever had, but it was _____.
3. There's a nice cafe _____ if you fancy a cup of tea.
4. Here's your pocket money. Remember you've got _____ all week!
5. We don't really like doing the tourist _____. We prefer to get _____.
6. Don't work too _____!
7. There's a cinema _____ where we live, so we go there at least once a month.
8. I've just treated myself to new boots, gloves and a woolly hat, so I'm really _____ winter now.

6. Transcript (255)   I: Interviewer   A: Anne

I: Um, you, you said when we met that um, you came to Sissi last year and you fell in love with it . . .

A: Mmm.

I: . . . and you decided to stay, so how, how did that actually happen?

A: Um, it, it wasn't so much Sissi. I fell, I fell in love with Greece a long time ago – my husband and I did. And we came on lots and lots of holidays and we always said that **(1) we would retire to Greece**, we always planned to do that. Um, and once we, we came and holidayed on, in Sissi and just loved it for . . . It is **(2) a holiday resort**, but it's still got that fishing village feel. The people are so beautiful here um, and that just made us decide we were going **(3) to make a go of it**. We were going to try and do it now and not when we retired. Um, I don't live in Sissi now, but I live not too far away, and obviously when I got the job with **(4) Olympic**, um, **(5) I begged them to put me down** in Sissi because I wanted to work here, 'cos I wanted, I wanted the people . . . I thought the people that holidayed here would share my idea of, of the . . . what it's like and how pretty it is, so I thought **(6) I would get on with the people that holidayed here**.

I: Right. And has it worked out?

A: Yeah, yeah. **(7) I've got no regrets.** Love it. Um, I live in a traditional village up the road, so I can get away from **(8) the holiday resort bit**, but it's so lovely. **(9) I can knock off** in the . . . at lunchtime and go to the beach, so I can do the tourist bit still, as well. Um, and it's just such a lovely lifestyle. Um, I have to work hard in the summer, um, but um, the winter is worth it 'cos I'm a village girl.

I: Mhm, mm.

A: Um, and get the real traditional bit there, but I still have time to socialise and enjoy the sun and the life, so yeah, no regrets.

I: What about your husband? Does he work here?

A: He works and he works in the tourist industry as well. He's not **(10) a full-time rep**, he does, he does a jeep safari, drives a jeep safari. Um, he also does some guiding work um, and he does a couple of pub quizzes round the area as well, so lots of different things, but again in the tourist industry.

I: Now the tourist season doesn't go on all year here, does it?

A: No.

I: So do you still get paid by your company in the winter?

A: No, I um . . . It's a seven . . . six, seven-month period um, that you get paid. It is just a, **(11) a short-term contract**. Um, I actually started work this year um, 21st March and I'll go right through to the end of October. So you've got to make enough money, basically, in the summer to, to get you through the winter if you stay here. A lot of, a lot of the reps that um, that come out from the UK, they will go back and they'll take temp, **(12) temp jobs** in offices and things like that, you know, over the winter if they want to come back, which a lot of them do.

I: Mhm, mm. But that must be quite **(13) hard** – to make that money from seven months last through the winter months?

A: Um, it is if . . . I think it is if you have um, **(14) an ex-pat lifestyle**. We don't. In the winter we're very much village people. It sounds strange, but we live like the villagers. We pick olives in the winter with our friends and they don't actually pay us, but they own the kafeneion, so they feed us. So we get, we get food when we're out picking anyway and then every night we're expected to go down to the kafeneion and we eat with the family.

I: Mhm, mm.

A: So our, our cost of living is minimal in the winter, so we don't have to make a massive amount.

I: Right. We . . . We've noticed um, prices have really gone up in Greece over the last few years – maybe since they introduced the euro.

A: Mhm. Yeah.

I: Um, prices for eating around the harbour or so are really quite expensive. But when you go inland then it's much, much cheaper.

A: Yeah. It is. It's the same anywhere. If you, if you're on a . . . in . . . if you're in a resort, if you're on the coastline, it's going to be . . . They know people, tourists are going to pay the money. If you go to any um, inland villages, even if **(15) they're more geared up to tourists**, you're going to pay less. But **(16) if you really get off the beaten track** um, I mean our kafeneion, for instance, I can eat, we can eat there, even when we pay, um, for sort of nine euros, with drinks and food and **(17) meze** because the Greeks won't pay . . .

I: No.

A: . . . that.

I: And yet for that we're, that's what we're paying for two sandwiches and a cup of tea at lunchtime.

A: Yeah. I mean Sissi, I think, is particularly expensive. It is seen as, as 'a nice place to, to holiday', and so the . . . you know, **(18) they have bumped their prices up a little bit.** (laughs)

I: It's understandable, really. Um, can I ask where you come from in the UK?

A: Um, **(19) I was brought up in Nottingham.** Um, I was actually born in Newcastle and all my family live up, up North, now, but um, before we moved out here my husband and I lived in Burton-on-Trent . . .

172   A Place I Know Well

I: Oh, right.
A: ... for, for nine years.
I: That's a lovely place, isn't it? You've got a big river going through ...
A: Yeah.
I: ... and all the beer-making companies.
A: Well, I used to work in the museum, the (20) Bass Museum ...
I: Oh, right. Very good.
A: Yeah, so I was involved in, in that side of it. Knew quite a lot of ... about it. But yeah, it is nice.

7. Words and Phrases

1. we would retire to Greece – when we finished our working lives we would spend our remaining years in Greece
2. a holiday resort – a place where people go on holiday
3. to make a go of it – to make a success of something, usually by working hard at it
4. Olympic – a holiday company
5. I begged them – I pleaded with them, as in 'Please can we stay up late tonight, Mummy, please, please, please?'
6. I would get on with the people – I would have a good relationship with these people
7. I've got no regrets – I know I made the right decision.
8. the tourist resort bit – all the touristy things such as sunbathing, swimming, etc.
9. I can knock off at lunchtime – I can finish work at lunchtime
10. a full-time rep – a full-time representative of a holiday company
11. a short-term contract – a legal agreement to work for a company for a fixed period
12. temp jobs – temporary jobs, i.e. jobs for a short period of time (as opposed to permanent jobs)
13. hard – difficult
14. an ex-pat lifestyle – the lifestyle of a British person who has gone to live in another country but who still does the same things, eats the same food, etc, as when s/he was in the UK
15. they're more geared up to tourists – they're more used to and experienced at dealing with tourists
16. if you really got off the beaten track – if you went to places away from the main roads and resorts where few tourists go
17. meze – a small Greek dish, usually served as an appetizer or as an accompaniment, or several *mezethes* may make up an entire meal
18. they have bumped their prices up a little bit – they have put up their prices
19. I was brought up in Nottingham – I grew up in Nottingham
20. Bass – a famous British company which makes a dark bitter beer

UNIT 14 Jill

1. Pre-Listening Comprehension

A Schema building

Jill is a nurse from North Wales. A few years ago she spent a year working in the USA. She lived in Bonsall, a small town near San Diego, in California. How much do you know about California? Circle the correct answer.

1. California is known as the **Golden State** / **Hollywood State** / **Blue State**.
2. A lot of people moved to California right after the discovery of **copper** / **silver** / **gold** there in 1848.
3. California is known for its beaches, mountains, wine regions, and amusement parks, and sits on the **east** / **west** / **south** coast of the United States.
4. San Diego is located in the southernmost part of California, near the border with **Mexico** / **New Mexico** / **Arizona**.

A Place I Know Well

B Discussion

Discuss the questions in small groups. Share your answers with the class.

1. Do you know anything else about California or San Diego?
2. Have you or has anyone in your family ever been to the USA, or do you have any family living there?
3. Do you know what a Welsh accent sounds like?

C Normalisation

(256)

NOTE: The interview takes place in a pub, so there is quite a lot of background noise. You may find this unit rather challenging, and need to repeat the audio tracks to aid your comprehension.

Jill talks about how she ended up working in the USA. This exercise is designed to help you get used to Jill's voice.

1. Where in the UK did Jill move to from North Wales?
2. What nationality was the man she was working for there?
3. Who did she look after?
4. How did Jill get to Sloane Street from Battersea?
5. Which bridge did she go over?
6. Which word does Jill use to describe the bridge?
7. In which US state was her boss living at the time?
8. What nationality was her boss's ex-wife?
9. How long did Jill go to the USA for?

2. Listening Comprehension

A Gap-fill

(257)

Jill talks about living in San Diego. Before you listen, try to predict which words, or which **types** of words will fit in the gaps. Then listen and check your answers.

1. Bonsall is in _____ San Diego County.

2. The ranch Jill lived on had a _____ _____.

3. When she got there, Jill's boss was planting _____ _____ and mulberry _____.

4. He was trying to _____ a garden from his homeland.

5. The ranch was out in the _____, so Jill had to learn to _____.

6. The ranch was about _____ _____ from the _____.

7. The nearest seaside town was called _____.

8. It has miles of sandy _____.

B True / False

(258)

Jill talks about going to the beach. Listen and decide if each statement is True (T) or False (F). Remember to give reasons for your answers.

1. _____ Jill used to work six days a week.
2. _____ Before she passed her driving test, Jill used to take the bus to Oceanside.
3. _____ Jill never used to go into the water.
4. _____ The sea was very warm.
5. _____ The ranch was 45 minutes' drive north of San Diego.

176   *A Place I Know Well*

C Gap-fill

Jill talks about spending her free time in a park in San Diego. As with Exercise A, try to predict which words, or which **types** of words will fit in the gaps. Then listen and check your answers.

1. San Diego is a big _____, but it has a nice _____ area with a lot of _____ and _____.
2. Balboa Park is where you can find all the _____ and _____ _____.
3. Jill says you could spend _____ going around Balboa Park.
4. She used to take a _____, lie on the _____ for a while and then go in and have a bit of _____.
5. Sometimes she'd take a _____ or go for a walk and look at all the _____.

D Questions

Jill talks about something that happened to her after her year in California. Listen and answer the questions.

1. What happened to Jill because she was swimming every day?
2. What kind of clothes did she wear in the USA?
3. What clothes did she put on the day she left for England?

Big Sur, California

UNIT 14: *Jill*

3. Features of a Welsh Accent and Informal Spoken English

A The *a* sound

(261)

Many people speak Welsh in Wales. In fact Jill is bilingual, as are all her family, most of whom have remained in North Wales.

A standard feature of both a North and South Welsh accent is a short *a* sound.

In this first exercise see if you can hear whether there's a difference between Jill's pronunciation of the following words containing *a*, and your teacher's pronunciation:

> *Different career path*
>
> *he looked after for years and years and years . . .*
>
> *she needed looking after*
>
> *It has a really big area called Balboa Park . . .*
>
> *all the museums and the art galleries*

Can you imitate Jill's pronunciation, just for fun?

B *'cos* for *because*

(262)

When we are talking quickly, we often say *'cos* instead of *because* as it's shorter and easier to say. Listen to Jill:

> *he looked after for years and years and years, 'cos that's what you do in that culture*
>
> *he decided he'd like his old nanny to go back and live with him and um, 'cos she needed looking after*
>
> *you don't realise, of course, 'cos it, it's so hot over there*

C Native speaker errors

Native speakers often make mistakes when they're talking quickly. Can you identify the mistakes Jill makes in these two excerpts?

> *I was um, working privately for a Iranian gentleman*
>
> *so by the time the year had finished and I had put on my jeans and jumpers to come home to England, which was in the October, I think, nothing fit me!*

A Place I Know Well

D actually

The word *actually* is used far more often in spoken English than in written English. Jill often uses *actually* when she is explaining things to the interviewer, as in these examples:

Int: *Where was this?*
Jill: *This was in London, actually.*

Jill: *He was planting fruit trees and mulberry bushes, which actually grow in Iran, apparently.*

Jill: *It has miles of sandy beaches, actually.*

Jill: *But it's so hot there that it's quite refreshing, actually.*

She also uses *actually* to correct the interviewer in a gentle way:

Int: *Was it right by the sea?*
Jill: *No, it wasn't. It was in the country, actually.*

Here are some more examples of this second usage of *actually* to gently correct someone:

Rosa: *That's a beautiful picture. Did you paint it yourself?*
Pam: *No, it's a print, actually.*

Pip: *I didn't know you spoke Swedish!*
Jan: *That was Danish, actually.*

Dan: *I owe you £20, don't I?*
Pat: *No, it's £30, actually.*

Aya: *It must take you ages to cycle to work.*
Art: *I can do it in less than 10 minutes, actually.*

Now try to come up with your own examples using *actually*.

> **IMPORTANT** Unlike *actuellement* in French, or *aktuell* in German, *actually* does not mean *currently* or *current*.

4. Further Language Development

A Extension exercise

Fill in the blanks in these new sentences with words you heard during Jill's interview. The words are listed in the box to help you.

> after   bridge   country   dearly   fit   gorgeous
> loose   nanny   opportunity   planting   profession
> refreshing   sandy   spend   used   weight

1. These trousers are a bit _____, so I'm just going to fetch a belt. I don't want them falling down in the middle of my speech.
2. The stream's too deep to wade across, but there's a little _____ a bit further on, so we can cross there.
3. We had a wonderful holiday, but the beach was a bit disappointing. They said it was _____, but when we got there it was really stony because they'd had a storm and all the sand had washed away.
4. I love my brother _____, but sometimes he drives me mad!
5. Can you look _____ the children while I pop out to the shops?
6. His parents both worked so he had a _____ when he was a little boy.
7. It's quite _____ to run cold water over your wrists on a hot summer's day.
8. We've got a flat in London and a little cottage in the _____, about 10 miles from the sea.
9. I've got the _____ to go and work in Russia for a year, but I'm not sure I want to go.
10. I really like this jacket, but it doesn't _____ me very well. The shoulders are a bit too wide and the sleeves are too short.
11. When I was a boy a group of us _____ to play football in that park every Saturday morning.
12. They say you need to _____ days going round the Hermitage Museum in St Petersburg, but we've only got an afternoon free, unfortunately.
13. Sarfraz is in the middle of _____ potatoes in the garden. Shall I get him to call you back?
14. That's a _____ coat! Where did you get it from?
15. You look fantastic! Have you lost _____?
16. I was an accountant by _____, but then I began painting 20 years ago and now I make a living doing that.

180   *A Place I Know Well*

B Colloquial English

Jill, like Scott, Ingse and Anne, uses a lot of colloquial English words and phrases in her interview. Colloquial English is found in informal spoken and written English, for example when friends chat or write emails. Fit the words and phrases in the box into the sentences below.

> a bit chilly   for a bit of a change   a lift   a lovely spot
> by profession   career path   in her old age   In fact
> in your culture   right by   see the sights

1. They've got a beautiful house in the country, _____ a river.
2. You don't have to go yet. _____ why don't you stay the night? We've got a spare bedroom.
3. Are you allowed to eat pork _____?
4. Let's go and _____ first, and then we can go and have lunch somewhere.
5. My grandmother loved dancing, even _____.
6. Why don't we try that new Sri Lankan restaurant _____?
7. Why don't we stop here? It's _____ for a picnic.
8. It's _____. Shall I put the fire on?
9. Basically he chose the wrong _____ when he was 18 and he's never been happy since.
10. Why don't I give you _____ as it's raining?
11. He used to be an accountant _____, but then he retrained as an osteopath in his 40s.

C Transformations

Change the word in each bracket which Jill used in her interview to form a word which fits the gap.

1. I decided on a career in (nurse) _____ when I was about 17.
2. She's very (thought) _____ – she never forgets anyone's birthday.
3. Economic (grow) _____ has been slowing in recent months.
4. The wind's coming from a (south) _____ direction, apparently.
5. Normally they serve (refreshing) _____ at half-time.
6. How much do you (weight) _____ now?
7. My cousin became a (profession) _____ tennis player at 17.
8. Hurry up! You need to make a (decided) _____.
9. We haven't moved yet, (actual) _____.
10. Have you (planting) _____ those tulip bulbs yet?

5. Transcript 🎧 263   I: Interviewer   J: Jill

I: OK. Now you went to live in America a few years ago, I think?
J: I did. I was um... I'm a nurse by profession and um, from North Wales, and I moved down to London. Bit of a change. **(1) Different career path.** And I was um, **(2) working privately** for a [sic – *an*] Iranian gentleman er, looking after his nanny, his childhood nanny, really. Looks after... he looked after for years and years and years, 'cos that's what you do in that culture. And er... **(3) he loved her dearly.**
I: So she'd looked after him when he was young and then he looked after her in her old age?
J: Yes. Yes, exactly.
I: OK.
J: So...
I: Where, where was this?
J: This was in London, actually. Um, Sloane... **(4) Sloane Street**, in fact. I used to travel every day um, from **(5) Battersea** – walk. It was really lovely, across the Albert Bridge, which is a beautiful bridge.
I: Mhm, hmm.
J: So... He came over one time, when... he, he was living in California and he decided he'd like his old nanny to go back and live with him and um, 'cos she needed looking after.
I: So who was she living with in London, then?
J: His ex-wife.
I: Oh, OK.
J: Who was American.
I: Right.
J: And um, so we all, we all went over. He asked, he asked me if I'd like to go over and look after her, nanny and er, yes, **(6) I gladly accepted.** I thought 'What an opportunity!'
I: Mhm, hmm.
J: And um, so off I went. I had a, a ticket er, for a year.
I: Mhm, hmm.
J: And er, we, we were living in a place called Bonsall, which is in San Diego County, northern San Diego County, and **(7) it was a lovely spot.** We lived on **(8) a ranch.** We had a swimming pool, **(9) all these grounds** and he, he, he hadn't been there that long so he was um, planting er, fruit trees and all sorts of other trees, **(10) mulberry bushes**, which actually grow a lot in Iran, apparently, but er, he was trying to recreate them...
I: Mhm, hmm.
J: ...in this place. And it, it was a beautiful spot.
I: Was it right by the sea?
J: No, it wasn't. It was in the country, actually, and er, so I had **to** learn to drive quite quickly.
I: But how far were you from the coast?
J: About, about 10 miles, I would say.
I: Mhm, hmm.
J: And er, it was a place called Oceanside. And it had er, miles of sandy beaches, actually. It's a lovely place. So I'd have one day off a week and er, **(11) he would give me a lift** into Oceanside before I'd learned to drive and er, spent all day on the beach, in the sea – **(12) gorgeous!** Quite **(13) heavy waves** – it's the Pacific and in fact er, it's quite **(14) chilly.**
I: Right.
J: But it's so hot there that it's, it's quite **(15) refreshing**, actually.
I: Did you use to go up to San Diego?
J: I did er, travel down to San Diego, in fact. It's about 45 minutes further south.
I: Right.
J: And er, which... In fact it's a, it's a big city, but it's really nice. It has **(16) a downtown area** er, which you can walk around – you know, all the usual shops and restaurants, etc. It has a really big area called Balboa Park which is er, er, **(17) lots of greenery** and that's where all the museums and the art galleries – that's... you... oh, days and days and days you could spend there if you wanted to.
I: Mhm, hmm.
J: And I, and I used to – take a book, you know. You'd lie on the grass for a little bit, go in **(18) and have a bit of culture**, then went out and have myself a picnic or something, just walk about looking at the sights, really.
I: Mhm, hmm.
J: Which was really nice.
I: You said about a swimming pool. Did you go swimming every day?
J: I did, in fact. Yes, I lost a lot of weight because I was doing it every day and you don't realise, of course, 'cos it, it's so hot over there and you're just wearing shorts and vests and T-shirts and things like this, so by the time the year had finished and I had put on my jeans and jumpers to come home to England, which was in the October, I think, nothing fit [sic – *fitted*] me! **(19) It was really loose!** And **(20) I hadn't realised**, but er, that was nice.

182   *A Place I Know Well*

6. Words and Phrases

1. **dif**ferent ca**reer** path – Jill had been working as a nurse in the NHS (National Health Service) in North Wales, but when she went to London she took a different career path and decided to work privately.
2. working **priv**ately – Jill was working for an employer, i.e. one person rather than an organisation
3. he loved her **dear**ly – he loved her very much
4. **Sloane** Street – a street which runs between Knightsbridge and Chelsea – two very expensive parts of central London
5. **Bat**tersea – a much less affluent area of London on the south bank of the River Thames
6. I **glad**ly ac**cept**ed – I was very happy to accept
7. it was a **love**ly spot – It was a very nice location
8. a ranch – a house on one level on a large plot of land
9. all these grounds – the large area of gardens and land surrounding the house
10. **mul**berry **bush**es – Bushes are plants with thin branches, smaller than trees, which grow in a rounded shape. Mulberry bushes have small, soft, purple fruit.
11. he would give me a lift into **O**ceanside – he used to drive Jill to Oceanside in his car
12. **gor**geous – beautiful
13. **hea**vy waves – Waves are raised lines of water which move across an area of water such as an ocean or the sea. Heavy waves are high waves which come in with a lot of force.
14. **chill**y – cold
15. re**fresh**ing – making you feel less hot
16. a down**town area** – the central part of the city
17. lots of **green**ery – lots of grass, trees and bushes
18. and have a bit of **cul**ture – and do something cultural such as visiting a museum, but not for long
19. It was **real**ly loose! – The clothes she's brought with her from London were now too big because she'd lost weight.
20. I hadn't **real**ised – Until this point Jill had not known how much weight she had lost.

UNIT 14: *Jill* 183

UNIT 15 Barbara

1. Pre-Listening Comprehension

A Schema building

Barbara was born and brought up in northern Germany. We heard her talking about her family in Unit 5. In this unit, she talks about Paderborn, the city where she lives.

How much do you know about Germany? Write T for True or F for False.

1. _____ East and West Germany reunified in 1980.

2. _____ The capital of Germany is Berlin.

3. _____ The population of Germany is smaller than the population of the UK.

4. _____ Germany comprises 16 states (Länder), such as Bavaria and Saxony, all with very distinct identities.

B Discussion

Discuss the questions in small groups. Share your answers with the class.

1. Do you know anything else about Germany?
2. How much do you know about the German language? Have you ever studied it?
3. Do you know what a German accent sounds like?

C Normalisation

The aim of this first exercise is to allow you to become accustomed to Barbara's voice. Listen to the first part of the interview and answer the following questions.

1. Which two adjectives does Barbara use to describe Paderborn?
2. How many people live there?
3. What religion are most of the inhabitants of Paderborn?
4. What has a big influence on Paderborn?

Paderborn Cathedral

2. Listening Comprehension

A Gap-fill
🎧 265

Barbara talks about things you can see in Paderborn. Before you listen, try to predict which words, or which **types** of words will fit in the gaps. Then listen and check your answers.

1. Paderborn has had a _____ since _____ .
2. There are quite a _____ of computer _____ in Paderborn.
3. Nixdorf used to be the _____ computer company in Germany.
4. Paderborn has the world's largest computer _____ .
5. Recently a _____ belonging to King _____ I was excavated near the cathedral, which is in the city _____ .
6. A _____ is held regularly _____ the cathedral.
7. There has been a market there _____ the Middle _____ .
8. The market takes place every _____ and _____ .
9. You can buy _____ and _____ at the market, as well as other things.

B True / False
🎧 266

Barbara talks about the market in Paderborn. Listen and decide if each statement is True (T) or False (F). Remember to give reasons for your answers.

1. _____ The fresh produce sold at the market comes from all over the world.
2. _____ Paderborn is surrounded by countryside.
3. _____ The area around Paderborn is quite hilly.
4. _____ A lot of foreigners live around Paderborn.
5. _____ Local farmers sell their produce at the market.
6. _____ Barbara enjoys going to the market.
7. _____ Barbara says the fruit and vegetables at the market are very cheap.
8. _____ Barbara always has to go straight home after she goes to the market.

3. Features of a German Accent and L1 Interference

A The *th* sound

267

The letters *th* found at the start of words such as *the* and *think* are difficult for German speakers to pronounce. Often they use the letter *s* instead.

Barbara speaks excellent English, but sometimes she says *s* instead of *th*, especially when she's speaking fast.

First listen to how she pronounces the first *th* of *thousand* correctly, but then carries this *th* sound over to the *s* of *thousand*, so that it sounds like *thouthand*:

Well, one hundred and twenty <u>thousand</u> by now.

B Listening for the *th* sound

268

In fact Barbara only uses the letter *s* instead of *th* six times during the interview out of the 40 words which contain the letters *th*.

Put a tick ✔ or a cross ✘ next to each word containing the letters *th* according to whether Barbara pronounces it correctly or incorrectly.

1. they ( ) are mostly Catholic ( )
2. What I really like is the ( ) market.
3. Well, we've got a university over there . . . ( )
4. the ( ) largest computer museum of the ( ) world
5. from the ( ) region
6. Very old, sort of Gothic ( ) cathedral. ( )
7. and they all bring their ( ) products to the ( ) market
8. It's great fun to be there...... ( )

UNIT 15: *Barbara*   **187**

C The present perfect with *since*

Native English speakers tend to use the present perfect simple or continuous with *since*, as in these examples:

> *I'm starving! I haven't had anything to eat since breakfast.*
>
> *I have lived here since 2006.*
>
> *I have been working non-stop since 9 o'clock.*

However, in many other languages (German, French, Swedish, Russian, etc.) speakers use the present simple with *since*. This is why Barbara uses *we've got* (meaning *we have*) in the following excerpt:

> *we've got a university over there since 1970*

It is also why she uses *must be*, rather than *must have been* in the following excerpt:

> *It must be like… that er, since the Middle Ages, I think.*

D The letter *u* in words such as *museum* and *computer*

(269)

Native British English speakers pronounce the letter *u* in words such as *museum*, *computer* and *music* with the sound of the letter *y* in front, whereas German speakers pronounce the letter *u* as in the sound a cow makes: *moo*. This can be heard in German words featuring the letter *u* – *Museum*, *Musik*, *Mutti*, etc.

Listen to how Barbara pronounces museum in the following excerpt:

> *The largest computer museum of [sic – in] the world.*

188   *A Place I Know Well*

4. Further Language Development

A Extension exercise

Fill in the blanks in these new sentences with words you heard during Barbara's interview. The words are listed in the box to help you.

> impressive   must   open-minded   region
> said   saying   since   symbol

1. We have a _____ in English: 'The early bird catches the worm.' What do you think it means?
2. Moscow is now _____ to be the most expensive city in the world.
3. I think the euro _____ looks too much like the dollar sign.
4. This inn has been here _____ the Middle Ages.
5. You _____ have been upset when you finished last in the Marathon.
6. My grandmother is very _____ – you can talk to her about anything.
7. Considering he's got so much money, you'd think he'd have a more _____ house.
8. This _____ of France is very famous for its cheese and its wine.

B Colloquial English

As with Scott, Ingsa, Anne, and Jill, Barbara uses a lot of colloquial English words and phrases in her interview. Colloquial English is found in informal spoken and written, for example when friends chat or write e-mails. Try to fit the words and phrases in the box into the sentences below.

> a a little bit of   in the world   quite a lot of
> quite famous for   to save money   to be honest

1. I'll just have _____ cake, please, 'cos I'm supposed to be on a diet.
2. I live in Walthamstow, which is _____ its William Morris Gallery.
3. I'm trying _____ this month 'cos I owe a lot of money on my credit card.
4. It's a very built-up area, but there are _____ trees around, which is nice.
5. Munich is my favourite city _____.
6. I'll just have a sandwich, thanks. I'm not very hungry _____.

UNIT 15: *Barbara*

5. Transcript

I: Interviewer **B:** Barbara

I: Um, I've never been to Paderborn. Can you tell me a little bit about it?
B: Well, Paderborn is a ... it really is a nice city. It's very quiet. It's got about ... one hundred thousand ... – well, one hundred and twenty thousand by now – inhabitants. And Paderborn is said to be very, very Catholic.
I: Right.
B: There's **(1) a saying in Germany**, there, to compare black – **(2) a symbol of Catholic** – you would say um, 'black', compare it to Mu ... Münster ...
I: Mmm.
B: ... top. Paderborn, so there.
I: The blackest ...
B: Blackest.
I: OK.
B: Yes. It really is a saying.
I: So most of the inhabitants are Catholic?
B: Yeah, they are mostly Catholic and er, the church has got a ... **(3) quite a big influence in town** – still has.
I: Mhm.
B: Well, we've got a university over there ...
I: Mmm.
B: ... since 1970.
I: Uh, huh.
B: And ... **(4) it's a bit more open-minded** now. It's not so traditional any longer. And we've got quite a lot of computer firms.
I: Mhm.
B: And er ... the very, the very ... Well, it was the biggest com ... German computer firm in ... was it started in Paderborn. It was called **(5) Nixdorf**. And um, we've got the ... what have we got? The largest computer museum of [*sic – in*] the world, they say. It really is **(6) very impressive** ...
I: Uh, huh.
B: ... to have it. And so we've got quite a lot of people working in the computer business ...
I: Mmm.
B: ... here now.
I: Right.
B: So it's computer and science ... and K ... church, really.
I: Mhm, hm. Is it a, a famous cathedral in Germany?
B: It's quite famous, yeah. Very old, sort of **(7) Gothic cathedral**. And it's got er, well, **(8) they've er, excavate** ... excavated a palace of ... King Charles. Charles the First ...
I: Mhm!
B: ... Charlemagne, you say?
I: Yes. Uh, huh.
B: ... quite near the cathedral, and so it's quite famous. Very old.
I: Mmm.
B: And um, it's in the city centre and ... What I really like is the market. We've still got a market just around the cathedral. It must be [*sic – must have been*] like ... that er, since **(9) the Middle Ages**, I think. Really good.
I: Is that every week, or ...
B: It's that every week. It's a Wednesday and Saturday market. And you can buy vegetables, fruit – everything you get from the, from the region, 'cos **(10) the region**, it's really very much countryside – very flat, a lot of farmers living around, and, and they all bring their **(11) products** [*sic – produce*] to the market.
I: Mhm.
B: It's very, very traditional.
I: So, do you go every Saturday, when you're not working?
B: Yeah. I love to do that. Well, you, you won't save money, but you ... **(12) it's great fun to be there** ...
I: Mhm.
B: ... fresh fruit and ...
I: So it, it's not cheap? It's, it's more expensive than a supermarket?
B: To be honest yeah, it is, yeah!
I: Mhm. OK.
B: Yeah.
I: But better quality.
B: Yeah. And you meet people. After that you have ... well, a coffee at the café. That's good.

190   *A Place I Know Well*

6. Words and Phrases

1 a saying – a well-known, short statement which expresses a idea which people believe is true and wise (often different from the simple meanings of the words it contains)
2 a symbol – a sign, shape, picture, etc. used to represent something else
3 quite a big influence – it has an effect on people
4 it's a bit more open-minded now – it's more open to new ideas than it used to be
5 Nixdorf – a famous German computer firm founded in Paderborn in 1952 which merged with Siemens in 1990 and then became Wincor Nixdorf in 1990
6 very impressive – something to be admired because it is very large, important, special, etc.
7 Gothic – a style of architecture common in Europe between the 12th and 16th centuries with pointed windows and arches, very high ceilings and tall, thin columns
8 they've excavated a palace – they have dug up a palace which was buried under the earth (a palace is a large, grand building and the official home of a ruling king, queen, bishop, etc.)
9 the Middle Ages – the period in European history between about 1100 AD and 1500 AD
10 the region – the area (here Barbara is referring to the area around Paderborn)
11 their products – products are things which are made to be sold (as opposed to produce, which refers to things grown or produced by farmers – vegetables, fruit, cheese, etc.)
12 it's great fun – it's very enjoyable

Collins

Also available in the
Real Lives, Real Listening series:

Elementary 978-0-00-752231-6

Advanced 978-0-00-752233-0

If you need help finding our books, please e-mail us at
collins.elt@harpercollins.co.uk.

www.collinselt.com   www.facebook.com/collinselt   @CollinsELT